Gothic vs. Classic

ARCHITECTURAL PROJECTS IN SEVENTEENTH-CENTURY ITALY

Gothic vs. Classic

ARCHITECTURAL PROJECTS IN SEVENTEENTH–CENTURY ITALY

Rudolf Wittkower

GEORGE BRAZILLER NEW YORK

This book was adapted for publication from the Charles T. Mathews Lectures, 1971–72 by George R. Collins and Margot Wittkower.

To Mario and Fiammetta, in whose Tuscan home many of these pages were written.

CONTENTS

PREFACE

I N HIS INTRODUCTORY REMARKS, Rudolf Wittkower explains why he chose the cathedrals of Milan, Bologna, and Florence to illustrate his thesis, and at the beginning of chapter I he gives his reason for the preeminence assigned to Milan in the story he has to tell—part of this reason being the extraordinary, and as yet not fully tapped richness of the *Archivio del Duomo*. Our work in the archive was so very enjoyable not only because of the many unexpected finds among the documents directly related to the history of the cathedral, but also because of the incidental glimpses afforded in the widest sense into the social history of Milan. Even the various stages in the cataloguing of the documents are revealing. The first attempt at ordering the miscellaneous papers was made as early as 1592, but really serious steps were taken only in 1742 when it was decided to create "an archive" as distinct from a mere collection. This task was entrusted to a worthy *avvocato* who devoted five years of love and labor to the ordering and registering of some two hundred and fifty of the most ancient papers and parchments. The turn from this antiquarian approach of the eighteenth century to the methodical procedure of the early twentieth century is well attested in the book *L'archivio della Fabbrica del Duomo di Milano, riordinato e descritto dal Dr. E. Verga*. Between his appointment as director of the archive in 1902 and the publication of his book in 1908 Dr. Verga had systematically reordered and catalogued the entire collection. Subsequent librarians have refined and elaborated what he began, so that today the archive is one of the best-kept and easiest sources of information a scholar may hope to find.

It may sound paradoxical, but one of the fascinations of the documents lies not so much in what they actually say, but in what they imply. As were all the Italian cities and states, Milan was constantly torn by wars, famine, plagues, and changes in government. The Viscontis and Sforzas came and went. There were brief French and Swiss interregnums. The Spaniards, who ruled from 1535 to 1713, were followed by the Austrians. Napoleon appeared on the scene in 1796 and governed, with one brief interval, until 1815, when the Austrians took over again. Foreign rule was finally ended in 1895. But nothing of this was ever allowed to interfere with the business of the cathedral. Whatever their private or political hopes or despairs may have been, generation after generation of Deputies to the Fabbrica met regularly and dutifully to plan, discuss, and resolve the problems entrusted to their care. Naturally, much of their time was taken up by financial matters. To this day the Milanese have a reputation for being generous and they certainly seem to have been so during the period with which this book is concernd. Petitions for higher salaries, demands for support of workmen's widows, extensions of leases for workshops handed down from father to son, or of church-owned grounds were usually granted and without too much delay.

On the other hand, the men in authority were keen businessmen, not easily swayed by aesthetic considerations. The open spaces around the cathedral, especially the square in front of it, were crowded with market stands and huts—for long an eyesore and an encumbrance. But the chapter drew rents from the stall-holders and it needed many petitions by "concerned" citizens before permission was given in 1682 to clear the piazza.

Reading the memoranda, the letters and bills, the carefully kept minutes of the meetings, one senses that time was of no consequence. Rather than take what might turn out to have been a hasty decision or an irrevocable step, one fell back on the never failing expedience: adjourn the meeting.

Into this world Napoleon burst in May 1796. Overnight the *Illustrissimi, Reverendissimi, e Colendissimi Signori Deputati* became *cittadini amministratori*—and with very reduced powers of administration to boot. Two committees concerned with constitutional and financial affairs had been installed, and the minutes of 7 August 1797 inform us that by order of the "general in capo Bonaparte" all matters relative to the continuation of the façade of the cathedral had to be put before those committees. Still, the time-honored deliberations go on aggravated by serious financial difficulties in which the Fabbrica now found itself. But here too Napoleon had the answer. On 17 July 1805 the deputies are informed that, according to a decree issued by "His Majesty," the Fabbrica has to sell property to the amount of 1,200,000 lire. Thus the final execution of the façade was secured.

But no imperial decree could change human nature. As before, artists were appointed and dismissed. Quarrels raged and were forgotten. Plans were made, discussed, and laid aside. And, incidentally, it had taken barely two years to turn the *cittadini amministratori* back into at least *signori deputati*.

Preface

The Charles T. Mathews Lectures Bequest, endowed in 1934, stipulates that a series of ten illustrated lectures on Gothic architecture be offered annually under the joint auspices of the School of Architecture of Columbia University and the Metropolitan Museum of Art in New York. With only five exceptions these lectures have been given each year since 1935. Considering the changes in taste over these almost four decades one might think that it would be increasingly difficult to find scholars prepared to present, and a public willing to attend, talks of such seemingly limited scope. Yet the variety of possible approaches to the problems offered by one of the great phases of our architectural heritage is such that the only concessions that have been made are to allow slightly more general medieval subjects and to cut down on the number of lectures. Instead of offering ten lectures of one hour each, they are usually now given as five longer sessions.

When Kenneth A. Smith, then Dean of the School of Architecture of Columbia University, invited Rudolf Wittkower in 1968 to give one of the Mathews series he accepted with alacrity. For quite some time he had been fascinated by a particular and hitherto all but neglected aspect of Gothic architecture. He wanted to find out what the great church builders and their patrons were thinking and doing when faced with the necessity of compromising between the Gothic past and the Classical-Baroque present in the later history of finishing major medieval churches.

After his retirement in 1969, Rudolf Wittkower began to sift his many, but rather haphazardly gathered notes, and started systematically to collect new material. The lectures were scheduled for the fall of 1971. From the outset he planned them as the nucleus of a future, more extensive publication, and for this reason he had already written the manuscripts for the lectures well ahead of time. But he was destined to present no more than the first of his five talks, suffering his fatal heart attack a few days before delivering the second.

The first lecture had already aroused great interest, however, and it was decided to present the lectures in full in the year after his death. Five of his former students and friends consented to read the lectures in the fall of 1972, and my warmest thanks go to Professor George R. Collins, Dr. C. Douglas Lewis Jr., Professor Henry Millon, Professor Craig Smyth, and Professor James S. Ackerman for their help and devotion in doing so. Professor Ackerman, moreover, provided a summing-up at the end in place of the one Professor Wittkower had begun, but which had been lost in the hurried effort to collect his papers from the several places where he had been working just before he was stricken. Each of the lecturers was kind enough to make constructive editorial suggestions regarding the lecture that he read. Professor Collins was unsparing with help in recovering and arranging the quantity of visual materials needed to illustrate the lectures.

I am equally indebted to the many friends in the Department of Art History and Archaeology at Columbia University, to Dean Smith of the School of Architecture, and the Avery Librarian Adolf K. Placzek for constant assistance and much personal encouragement. My thanks also go to Thomas P. F. Hoving, Director of the Metropolitan Museum of Art, to Suzanne Gauthier who took charge of all the technical arrangements at the museum with cheerful efficiency, and to Professor Cesare Gnudi, Bologna, who helped with photographic material needed for Chapter IV.

The response to Rudolf Wittkower's last work in its unusual mode of presentation was gratifying. It encouraged me to hope that it would be acceptable in print, too. Again it was George Collins who helped. Despite many other duties, he always found time to assist me in the preparation of the text and illustrations for publication; his son Lucas M. Collins did much of the photographic work. I wish I could find adequate words to express my gratitude to my coeditor. Never was the often-used phrase truer: without him this book would never have been printed.

I should like to put it on record that without the unstinting support in Milan of Professor Maria Luisa Gatti Perer, Director of the *Instituto per la storia dell'arte lombarda,* and the Rev. Monsignor Angelo Ciceri, director of the *Archivio del Duomo,* we would never have been able to achieve as much as we did in the all-too-brief time at our disposal. Even before our arrival in Milan, Professor Gatti Perer had thoughtfully prepared all the material she anticipated we might need, and during our stay she put all the resources of her institute, including a mass of photographic material, at our disposal in the most liberal way. Monsignor Ciceri was equally generous in allowing us unlimited use not only of the archive and the library, but also of all available tables which his untiring staff piled high with tome after ancient tome. I know that my husband would have wished to express his most sincere thanks to all of them.

In conclusion I should like to add a word about our editorial procedure. The author was left no time to revise his manuscript with his usual care. We therefore took it upon ourselves to even out an occasional stylistic roughness and to replace referrals to slides and lectures with references to illustrations and chapters. Otherwise the text of this book is exactly the same as that of the lectures.

The footnotes presented some problems. Rudolf Wittkower left several well-filled folders with notes, excerpts, book titles, and first brief sketches of his own ideas. It was not always easy to determine which were his own words and which were sources he had actually used or merely recorded, nor could I always be sure whether he had, in fact, read or only meant to read the books on his lists. I therefore abstained from appending a bibliography and provided footnotes only in cases where I was fairly sure to quote the correct source. Any error in this respect is entirely mine. A similar difficulty arose over the illustrations. The photographs and negatives used were not always sufficiently inscribed. I have done my best to trace their origins and if I have failed in one or the other case, I can only offer my sincere apologies.

New York   MARGOT WITTKOWER
November, 1973

INTRODUCTION

FOR MOST OF US who have been involved in the study of this subject, latter-day Gothic styles in architecture have meant the Gothic revival of the nineteenth century, and we have explained them as part of the romantic, medievalizing, liturgical, archaeological, or historicist propensities of that era. Here in Rudolf Wittkower's lecture-essays, however, we see the post-medieval Gothic style as a current architectural phenomenon in a part of Europe—Italy—that had developed a precocious aesthetic consciousness of what Gothic architecture was, and had done so largely because of a distaste that the maturing classical Renaissance had engendered for the *maniera tedesca.*

Although it is generally understood that the Gothic style flourished until late in northern Europe, that it entered a new "purist" phase in sixteenth-century Spain, and that it never really terminated in England at all, how many of us know that Gothic façades for important Italian churches were designed by artists like Peruzzi, Giulio Romano, and Vignola in the sixteenth century, Juvarra and Vanvitelli in the eighteenth, and that Bernini had discoursed seriously on the virtues of one Gothic design over another? Such disputes as Bernini was drawn into regarding the proper way in which the Cathedral of Milan was to be finished agitated local authorities in Italy throughout the entire Renaissance and Baroque periods, occasionally requiring the intervention of the Vatican itself to adjudicate.

Professor Wittkower has divided his analysis of the fluctuating currents of Gothicism and Classicism in Italy into several topics. He deals, although not in this order, with four model controversies: (1) over the façade of the Duomo in Florence, which was designed in classical terms during the sixteenth and seventeenth centuries and was built as Gothic in the nineteenth; (2) over the Gothic vaulting of the interior of San Petronio in Bologna, which provoked a pitched battle in the sixteenth century and was constructed in the seventeenth; (3) over the designs for the façade of San Petronio which went from Gothic to Classic and back to Gothic during the sixteenth and seventeenth centuries, but were never built; and (4) over the façade of the Cathedral of Milan where, after a classical interlude around the year 1600, the Fabbrica agonized over various Gothic alternatives until Napoleon put a stop to the matter and had it carried out as we see it today. The final and culminating topic of these essays is an evaluation of the considerable debt that such radical Baroque architects of Italy as Borromini and Guarini owed both to a taste for the Gothic and to Gothic building practices. From Leonardo and Bramante to Napoleon Bonaparte, Professor Wittkower informs us, the Gothic was alive and well in Italy and almost constantly engaged in a rough-and-tumble with the Classic.

The most crucial phase of this dialectic occurred during the seventeenth century, and it is on that century, as his title indicates, that the author dwells at greatest length. The long-drawn-out story of the completion of the façade of Milan Cathedral occupies three of the five chapters or lectures of which his study is composed. We are not surprised at this emphasis, because one of the characteristics of Rudolf Wittkower as a scholar and teacher was, when not dispelling misunderstandings about well-known periods of art history, to study neglected subjects that would cast new and vital illumination on their times. So it is with the story of the completion of the Cathedral of Milan. There exists an enormous cathedral archive and a number of partial studies have appeared, but it took his profound knowledge of the period and his remarkable synthesizing ability to set the many protagonists in proper motion across the Baroque stage of time. The related dramas of San Petronio in Bologna and the Duomo in Florence, more extensively published perhaps but scarcely familiar, play out a sort of entr'acte.

Particularly because of Professor Wittkower's experiences with the Milan archives, he is able to give us many details as to how a great civic building project operates. The structure of its administration, the interminable disagreements—aesthetic, financial, procedural, petty—are revealed, characterized, and related to prime architectural problems of the day. How, for instance, did the plethora of theorists who intervened manage to relate the "propriety" of Vitruvius to the "disordered" style of the Goths?

What we are provided with in these essays is a sort of paradoxical history of architecture: an analysis of the Renaissance and Baroque periods in terms of their antithesis, the Gothic. We see that Mannerist Italy tolerated Gothic designs, that the early Baroque (before and after 1600) went austerely and monumentally classical. By 1640 odd mixes and eccentric Gothic projects emerge. In the eighteenth century it all goes a little mad, but by about 1800 things become correctly historicist. That date marks the end of an era and essentially closes his story. Hopefully, someone will now continue with a study in depth of the early nineteenth-century competition for the cathedral façade in Florence and the late nineteenth-century one for rebuilding the façade in Milan—both of which events form part of that other, more familiar subject: the Gothic Revival.

GEORGE R. COLLINS

CHAPTER I

The Cathedral of
Milan: Prelude

I n 1960, Paul Frankl published a work entitled *The Gothic, Literary Sources and Interpretations through Eight Centuries.* It is a tome of over nine hundred pages that begins with Abbot Suger's mid-twelfth-century treatises and follows the theme through the centuries to modern interpretations of the Gothic style by such art historians as Henri Focillon, Ernst Gall, Dagobert Frey, Jean Bony, and Hans Sedlmayr. When one turns the pages of Frankl's book, one has the feeling that everything of interest and importance has been covered by a fine mind who devoted a large part of a long life to gaining a balanced assessment of opinions about Gothic architecture in all ages and countries.

Upon consideration, however, it appears that some periods are perhaps treated all too briefly: Frankl has less than thirty pages on views about the Gothic style in France, Italy, and Spain between the years 1530 and 1600 and less than fifteen pages on the same countries in the seventeenth century. But it would seem—and I hope to prove— that the late sixteenth and the seventeenth centuries are of exceptional importance in sorting out the problems that the legacy of the Gothic period posed to the central European countries.

The main title and the subtitles of the present work indicate that I shall not attempt to compete with my friend, Professor Henry-Russell Hitchcock, who began his series of Mathews lectures in 1970 with a broad presentation of the Gothic Revival of the eighteenth century from Bohemia to England. His main concern was to acquaint the audience with a great number of buildings. By contrast, I shall limit myself to a few, a very few, buildings, or rather projects, which I want to discuss in considerable detail. This limitation was forced upon me by my desire to explore what was going on in the minds of some of those who were trying to design and think "Gothic" in the seventeenth century. Thus, unlike Professor Hitchcock, I cannot unfold a vast panorama of buildings because of my time-consuming method of investigating selected cases in some depth.

In chapter one, I propose to lay the groundwork for the rest of the book, and I will not, at that point, enter into the seventeenth-century controversies. Let me mention straight away that, although my focus will indeed be the seventeenth century, we will have to look back in time and also take the story forward into the eighteenth and even the nineteenth and twentieth centuries.

It would be interesting to follow up the survival of Gothic conventions into and through the seventeenth century outside Italy —there is a recognizable Gothic undercurrent going on through the entire period here under review, mainly in the northern countries, in Germany and England. A great deal about Gothic in the seventeenth century might be learned by a close study of the attitudes that made such survivals possible, but this will not be developed here. On the other hand, a focus on Italy has its special rewards, because it is there that we can expect to find the most pointed and revealing views on Gothic. The reasons are obvious. Italy led Europe intellectually and artistically until the end of the seventeenth century. Only in fifteenth-century Italy was a conscious, programmatical, and forceful break with Gothic traditions accomplished; it was only there that the rise of the Renaissance was accompanied by an art theory that took its bearings from the authors of classical antiquity; and it was only there that a vision of historical evolution arose and took root, according to which the long period between the fall of the Roman Empire and the rise of the Renaissance appeared as a period of decline caused by barbaric invasions. All this would seem to be a clear pointer to the Italian approach to the Gothic style in the post-medieval period. Frankl called his chapter covering the Renaissance and Baroque era (i.e., the centuries from the fifteenth to the early eighteenth): "The Period of Reaction against Gothic." Indeed, a long book could be compiled from quotations of literary criticism of the Gothic style during those centuries. There was probably no Italian architect of importance during the sixteenth and seventeenth centuries whose terms of reference were other than classical. Nevertheless, we shall find that occasionally compelling circumstances arose in which Gothic projects superseded classical ones.

In order to get a feeling for the situation, one turns, of course, to the father of art-historical writing, Giorgio Vasari, whose *Lives of the Artists* appeared first in 1550 and, much amplified, in 1568. Vasari not only skillfully summarized the Italian approach to Gothic as it had developed over the previous hundred years but added to it a personal note of strong prejudice; he also had a formative influence on the opinions of later generations. Vasari expressed his considered opinion on Gothic—which at his time was called interchangeably *maniera tedesca* (German manner) and Gothic manner—in the celebrated introduction to his *Lives*.

After discussing the classical orders, Vasari turns to the work known as German, which, he tells his readers, is now avoided by the best architects "as monstrous and barbarous, and lacking everything that can be called order. Nay it should rather be called confusion and disorder." This idea is of central importance and we shall later consider the specific meaning of the concepts of order and disorder in the sixteenth and seventeenth centuries. Vasari then enumerates a great deal of Gothic detail which shows that he had studied Gothic buildings rather carefully (figs. 1, 2). "Doorways [he informs us] are ornamented with columns which are slender and twisted like a screw, and cannot have the strength to sustain a weight, however light it may be. Also on all the façades . . . they build cursed little niches, one above the other, with no end of pinnacles and points and leaves . . . so that it appears impossible that the parts should not topple over at any moment." He goes on to discuss the endless projections and breaks and corbellings and flourishes that throw the architects' work all out of proportion; "and often, with one thing being put above another, they reach such a height that the top of a door touches the roof. This manner [he concludes] was the invention of the Goths, for, after they had ruined the ancient buildings, and killed the architects in the wars, those who were left constructed the buildings in this style. They constructed pointed arches, and filled all Italy with these abominations of buildings . . . their style has been totally abandoned. May God protect every country from such ideas and style of buildings!"

One has to acknowledge that Vasari gave a shrewd characterization of the Gothic style, though its appreciation was marred by an almost physical aversion. Vasari's strictures on Gothic are encountered in many passages of his writings. In the same introduction from which

I have quoted, he mentions that "in our time certain vulgar architects . . . have worked . . . almost as if by chance, without observing decorum, art, or any order; all their things are monstrous and worse than the Gothic ones." Or to give another example: in order to underline emphatically his dislike of Antonio da Sangallo's wooden model of St. Peter's in Rome, a model that was harshly criticized by Vasari's adored master Michelangelo, he says that it reminds one "of the style and manner of the Germans rather than of the good manner of the ancients which the better architects nowadays follow."

Vasari's approach to the Gothic manner was, however, more complex than would appear from the remarks quoted here. It was Erwin Panofsky who first observed a strange paradox or seeming contradiction in Vasari's attitude. Vasari had been an avid collector of drawings, a fair number of which are still known: they are to be found in many great collections all over the world and are easily identifiable by the carefully rendered framing devices which Vasari himself designed for each of them. One of the treasures of his collection was a fourteenth-century drawing showing many small figures (now in the Bibliothèque de l'Ecole des Beaux-Arts in Paris) ascribed by Vasari to Cimabue and for which he designed a Gothic frame (fig. 3). In 1930 Erwin Panofsky dedicated to this phenomenon one of his penetrating investigations, which he entitled "The First Page of Giorgio Vasari's 'Libro.' A Study on the Gothic Style in the Judgment of the Italian Renaissance."

Two points made by Panofsky are of specific interest in the present context. First, with psychological insight he recognized that it was precisely the opposition to the Middle Ages that enabled the Renaissance—as he says—"to confront Gothic art, and thereby, even though through glasses tinted by hostility, to *see* it for the first time . . . as an alien and contemptible, yet for this very reason truly characteristic, phenomenon which could not be taken too seriously." Panofsky concluded that the North, "for want of distance, needed a long time . . . to understand Gothic works as manifestations of a great and serious style [while] the very enmity toward the Gothic established the basis for its recognition in Italy." Secondly, he emphasized that the problem of stylistic unity loomed large from the beginning of the Renaissance on. Thus, briefly, Vasari's knowledge of Gothic stylistic features, combined with the demand for stylistic consistency, determined his Gothic frame for the so-called Cimabue drawing.

This last point—stylistic consistency throughout a work—is a point to which we shall have to return constantly, and it therefore deserves some elaboration. We have to turn back to the great Leon Battista Alberti, writer, philosopher, artist, and architect, who often had an almost hallucinatory faculty for giving the stamp of finality to thoughts that moved his age. He answered the central question of Renaissance aesthetics, the definition of beauty, in a splendid phrase in his *Ten Books on Architecture,* written about 1450: harking back to Vitruvius, he declared beauty to consist in the harmony and concord of all the parts of a building ("concinnitas universarum partium"). This meant, of course, that when a Renaissance architect had to finish an older, pre-Renaissance building, the old and new parts had to be carefully reconciled. How Alberti himself interpreted this principle in practice is best illustrated by his façade of S. Maria Novella in Florence (fig. 4). When he began work on this façade in 1458 he found there a medieval colored marble incrustation (white panels framed by green bands), medieval tombs in Gothic recesses and even blind arcades resting on high pilasters. His own additions—mainly the superimposed columns, the attic, the classical pediment, and the large scrolls—blend so perfectly with the older parts that until recently the old and new parts had not been clearly distinguished by scholars.

Architects of the sixteenth and seventeenth centuries, too, were faced with this same problem: the harmonizing of older (Gothic) parts with later additions. The two supreme examples in Italy are the Cathedral of Milan and S. Petronio at Bologna. While S. Petronio has attracted some attention, in Italy as well as abroad, the problems of the Cathedral of Milan, in any case those with which we shall be dealing, have remained an almost strictly Italian art-historical concern.

So it is the Cathedral of Milan that will engage us first at some considerable length (figs. 5, 7). It is hardly necessary to mention that Milan Cathedral is one of the most sumptuous as well as one of the largest churches of the world. In fact, I believe that its length of about 500 feet and its greatest height of about 350 feet are surpassed only by St. Peter's in Rome. Well over three thousand statues found a home in Milan Cathedral, two-thirds of them on the exterior. Milan probably had the most extensive sculpture workshop of any cathedral; moreover, it remained in operation for almost half a millennium. The history of this vast enterprise, vast even by New York skyscraper standards, is extremely well documented—down to the minutest details.[1] Even such absurd and irrelevant facts as the death in 1660 of a hermit who had pitched his primitive abode on the roof of the cathedral is circumstantially recorded. Disconcertingly, however, sometimes the answers to our most pressing questions cannot be found.

Between 1877 and 1885 the administration of the cathedral published eight large volumes of documents from its archive.[2] These documents were selected with great discrimination, but represent only a fraction of the material available, especially for the seventeenth and eighteenth centuries. My wife and I had the good fortune of spending an intense period of work in that splendidly organized archive and the following remarks are based both on the published *Annals* and on our own finds. Of course, the early history of the cathedral was published more fully in the *Annals* and is much better known than the later periods of the history of the structure. Of the early period I shall only mention what we need as a background for later events.

The foundation of the present cathedral dates back to 1386, when it was decided to replace the old cathedral of S. Maria Maggiore by a modern and much larger building (figs. 10, 12). Right at the beginning an organization was created that was responsible for all aspects of building procedure and was called (as always in cases of Italian cathedrals) *Veneranda Fabbrica del Duomo*—the Reverend Fabric of the Cathedral. This organization still survives and now occupies a huge palace to the east of the choir of the church. As early as 1387 the bylaws of the Reverend Fabric were laid down and with some adjustments, mainly in 1564, they remained in force until 1902.

Briefly, the body responsible for the running of building matters was the "Consiglio di Fabbrica," the Council of the Fabbrica, which was at first run by some clerics and by noblemen and lawyers, reinforced by up to a hundred deputies recruited from citizens of good standing. This large general congregation met the first Sunday of every month, if possible, under the chairmanship of the Archbishop of Milan; here the grand strategy was thrashed out. The daily chores—such as watching over the conduct of workmen, assessing the quality of materials, looking into expenses, etc.—were administered by a team of four, three of whom changed weekly. As time went on, the power of the weekly deputies increased, and individual functions were more clearly defined. In the Constitution of 1564, for instance, the duties of the architect or engineer (as he was called) of the cathedral were spelled out in some detail, and there is a further definition of his office in a pamphlet of 1642 entitled "Il Governo della Fabbrica del Duomo di Milano"[3] (The Administration of the Fabbrica of the Cathedral). He or his assistant had to be day and night in the studio of the Campo Santo (directly east of the cathedral; of course the area was no longer used as a cemetery). He had to supervise the work of the masons, had to assess costs, the value of materials, and the quality of the work that had been finished; above all, he was responsible for designs and models and had to answer all questions that turned up at the meetings of the Fabbrica, and so forth.

This brief indication of the part played by council and committee deliberations and decisions in the erection of Milan Cathedral may come as a surprise. The fact is that often the slowness of progress in Milan was not the result of technical backwardness or incompetence, but was due primarily to the cumbersome organizational machinery set up for the control and running of the enterprise. It was this machinery that led to indecision, to procrastination, to constant changes of planning; remarkably often it led to obsessive suspicions, to prolonged court cases over which one forgot to get on with the job, and to the sudden dismissal of perfectly honest, honorable, and capable architects.

All this can be observed right from the start. The initial Milanese project had scarcely been adopted when the Council decided to summon an expert from Paris. He—Nicolas de Bonaventure—lasted just about a year, from 1389 to 1390. He was succeeded by the German Annas de Firimburg (or John of Freiburg) whose stay was even briefer. Meanwhile a mathematician, Gabriele Stornaloco, was summoned from Piacenza in September 1391; he submitted a drawing that still survives. The search among foreign experts went on. In November 1391 Heinrich Parler of Gmünd in southern Germany reached Milan; he stayed until July 1392. More foreigners, more crises. With the arrival of the Frenchman Jean Mignot in 1399 there seemed to be some progress; he first impressed his Italian patrons, but animosity soon built up against him. Accused of extravagance, he was dismissed in October 1401. He was the last foreigner employed by the Fabbrica and from then on the structure made such quick progress that its high altar was consecrated by Pope Martin V in 1418.

The story of the rapid changeover from one non-Italian architect to the next in the first fifteen years of the cathedral's history has often been told, above all, in an excellent paper by Professor James Ackerman.[4] Yet there is room for some further observations. The gentlemen of the Fabbrica were seeking enlightenment on two interrelated problems: they wanted expert opinion on questions of statics and on proportion. For them, as for other cathedral builders, it was a sine qua non that an overall, cohesive geometrical pattern be adopted to which the design had to conform. It was the geometrical scheme that, in their view, helped to ensure stability. The mathematician Stornaloco favored triangulation (fig. 20): equilateral triangles were to determine a grid system and all the essential points of the planning. Heinrich Parler suggested a plan *ad quadratum*, i.e., a grid system of squares, into which the height and width of aisles and nave had to be fitted (fig. 21). The Milanese, however, were not satisfied. From their Lombard point of view they found in both cases the height of the nave excessive and disturbing. They could not simply say: "Well then, let's build the nave lower." For them the beauty and solidity of the structure were closely allied to its geometry. So after they had started building according to Stornaloco's triangulation and reached the height of the outer piers, they decided to switch over to another geometrical system, namely to the so-called Pythagorean triangle that would allow them to build a lower nave (fig. 22). They probably did not mind sacrificing geometrical unity, because the Pythagorean triangle enjoyed a special reputation; its unique properties had been discovered by the Greeks and had remained known through the centuries: the sides of this triangle are related as 3:4:5 and thus form an arithmetical progression. No other right-angle triangle with this property can be constructed. Moreover, Vitruvius (whose work was also consulted during the Middle Ages) had given particular sanction to this Pythagorean invention (fig. 23).

Although it may be argued that this Milanese procedure represented a compromise and was inconsistent, at least from the standpoint of strict adherence to a unified geometrical system, the Cathedral has always been acclaimed for having been constructed in accordance with lucid mathematical principles. What Vasari called "confusion and disorder" would not apply here. There was an order embedded in the laws of geometry, and one had to admit that the principle of mathematical order, the one and all of Renaissance aesthetics, had here been followed. This point of view one encounters more than once in the seventeenth century and this helps us to understand why Gothic appeared acceptable for the cathedral.

An important link between the early building period and the seventeenth and eighteenth centuries' approach to the cathedral can be seen in Cesare Cesariano's edition of Vitruvius, published at Como in 1521. This grandest Vitruvius edition of the Renaissance was always revered not only because of its exceptional beauty, but also because of its intellectual prestige, for Cesariano had been a pupil of Bramante in Milan and many passages of his commentary seemed to echo the great master's mind. Now Cesariano illustrated the passage of the second chapter of Vitruvius' First Book, where the ancient author discusses plan, elevation, and perspective view of a building, with representations of Milan Cathedral (figs. 24, 25). Cesariano does not state explicitly what moved him to this extraordinary inclusion of a Gothic building in the classical text. But the illustrations are in a way self-explanatory. They manifest the pride of the humanist architect in the architectural geometry of this monumental structure.[5] The reign of triangulation, of the square, and of the circle—the latter two absolute essentials of classical and Renaissance aesthetics—demonstrated the validity of Late Gothic geometry, "Germanico more" (as Cesariano put it), within a classical Vitruvian system. As already stated, Cesariano's positive assessment of the great Gothic cathedral did not pass unnoticed. Luigi Vanvitelli's project for the façade of Milan Cathedral of 1745 (fig. 28), with a superimposed geometrical analysis by Karl Noehles,[6] clearly demonstrates Vanvitelli's dependence on Cesariano; and the section of Milan Cathedral published by François Blondel in his *Cours d' Architecture* of 1683 is obviously dependent on Cesariano and even shows the same triangulation system entered in dotted lines (fig. 29).

The checkered history of the construction of the cathedral will not be dealt with here. Art historically speaking, the two most exciting features of the church are the dome or tower and the façade. During the fifteenth century, models of the tower over the crossing, the *Tiburio*, as the Italians call it (fig. 6), were made by various architects; even a master from Strasbourg was consulted. A review of existing designs, probably dating from the late 1480s, survives and, for valid reasons, is usually attributed to Bramante.[7] Among the points Bramante raised in his memorandum the "conformità con il resto del edificio" (conformity with the rest of the building, i.e., once again the question of stylistic unity) played an important part, and he recommended a way of avoiding, as he expressed it, "disrupting the order [by which he means the style] of the edifice." Among others, Leonardo was invited to submit plans for the *Tiburio;* some of his sketches survive[8] and show that he suggested an octagonal structure with concave buttresses and slender pinnacles at the exterior, and intersecting arches inside (figs. 30, 31), indicating that he, too, was seeking conformity with the Late Gothic style of the cathedral. The inside of the dome and the octagonal drum outside with high Gothic windows were finished in 1500 (fig. 14). The *Tiburio* remained in this condition for 250 years —until 1762, when the model of the concave buttresses and the tall spire made by the cathedral architect, Francesco Croce, was approved and executed (fig. 9). It was not until 1774 that the crowning statue of the Virgin was placed over the finished *Tiburio*.

To turn now to the main topic of this chapter, we note that the first model of the cathedral probably had no façade. It is even unlikely that a façade project was in existence by 1521 or else the well-informed Cesariano would have illustrated it. It would seem that the planning of the façade was not seriously begun until the fourth decade of the sixteenth century, because in 1534 we find for the first time a deliberation requesting a concentration of interest upon the façade;[9] at last, in 1537, a young architect, Vincenzo Seregni, submitted a project of which, however, only the plan is presently known (figs. 15, 32). This plan (now in the Bianconi Collection in the Castello Sforzesco in Milan) shows two massive square towers jutting out in front of a relatively narrow façade with three entrance doors. Although Seregni's elevation is not known, one may make a pretty convincing guess regarding its style. In a letter accompanying his project, Seregni declared that the project conformed with the intentions of the founders of the cathedral.[10] Thus conformity—and this meant a Gothic façade—was on his mind. There are other indications in support of this conclusion.

Ever since 1503 the planning of the portal of the north transept (the "porta verso Compito"—as it was called: Compito was the name of the street running along the north side of the cathedral) was vigorously pursued. Nevertheless, the planning and replanning dragged on practically through the entire sixteenth century. Between 1534 and 1537 Seregni submitted a project (still in the archive of the Fabbrica) for the north transept wall and portal (fig. 33): it is a curious late-Gothic affair; the architecture of the portal itself is scarcely related to its superstructure; this part is closely reminiscent of German Late Gothic altar-shrines. Shortly later Seregni seems to have been able to offer a much more coordinated Gothic design. In any case, this may be deduced from the woodcut of the north transept front on a broadsheet of which only one copy survives in the Ambrosiana (fig. 34). To see such designs in proper perspective, it must be remembered that they were made shortly before Michelangelo became architect of St. Peter's.

In 1547 Seregni's dream came true: he was appointed Architect to the Cathedral,[11] but had to play second fiddle under his teacher Cristoforo Lombardo until, after Lombardo's death in 1555, he was put in sole charge. Although he maintained his position for two decades in all, his period of office was less successful than he had reason to expect. In July 1567 he was summarily dismissed although he was not yet old and, in fact, had still twenty-seven years to live—

he was dismissed, it would seem, as the direct result of near-revolutionary events in Milan.[12]

In 1560 Pope Pius IV had made his nephew, Charles Borromeo, then twenty-two years old, Cardinal Archbishop of Milan. The voices of critics were soon silenced, because this young man rapidly developed into one of the greatest churchmen of all time. He was canonized as early as 1610. The young archbishop was first needed in Rome and directed his diocese from there. It was only in 1565 that he settled permanently in Milan, where he displayed an immensely vigorous activity during the last nineteen years of his brief life. As a leading spirit of the Catholic Counter-Reformation and as one of the most energetic participants in the proceedings of the last years of the Council of Trent, he held determined views about the part that art and architecture ought to play in the process of rejuvenation of the Church. In 1577 he published a book entitled *Instructions for Ecclesiastical Buildings*, the only work that endeavored to apply the decrees of the Council of Trent to architecture. His recommendations are matter-of-fact, straightforward, practical, and without any abstract speculations. Nor does he touch upon aesthetic matters, and the words "style" or "*maniera*" (manner) do not occur. Nevertheless, it is certain that he admired the Roman basilicas of the Early Christian period; he himself was titular cardinal of one of them, S. Prassede. We may also be certain that for a leader of the Counter-Reformation the *maniera tedesca*, the German style, was emotionally unacceptable, for this was the style which the heretics north of the Alps applied to their churches.

Thus, one would expect that St. Charles had no use for Seregni's fondness for Gothic designs and that he wanted an architect who would be capable of translating his ideas into reality. Strangely enough, his choice fell on a painter—one who had made a name for himself—namely Pellegrino Tibaldi, in Italy usually called Pellegrino Pellegrini. Pellegrini was born in a small town in Lombardy in 1527, but grew up in Bologna and spent over three years in Rome, from 1549 to 1553. This early experience had a decisive influence upon his career. He was particularly captivated by the work of Michelangelo, whose influence permeates his own work as a painter. St. Charles Borromeo met him at Bologna in 1560 and must have formed a high opinion of his ability. In 1564 the Cardinal Archbishop called him to Milan, and for two decades Pellegrini enjoyed the full confidence of the great prelate. Pellegrini's first extensive work in Lombardy was the remarkable Collegio Borromeo at Pavia. Begun in 1564, the huge building displays a most powerful style for which there are no exact parallels in Rome. Before long Pellegrini was the most sought-after architect in Lombardy. On 7 July 1567—four days after Seregni's dismissal—he was elected Architect to the Cathedral,[13] no doubt owing to St. Charles's personal intervention. It would seem (and later events also show) that the archbishop had steered the dismissal of the one and then the take-over by the other, who had proved to be an immensely resourceful man and whose name seemed to be a guarantee for a resolute pursuance of the affairs of the cathedral. St. Charles was a shrewd judge of men, but—as we will see—he had not fully anticipated the consequences of his action.

First it must be said that under Pellegrini the building progressed very rapidly indeed. The side altars and the new main altar, the baptistery, the presbytery and the crypt, the pulpits and the floor of the cathedral, stained glass windows, and many other things were accomplished during his regime and from his designs: all classical. But the problem that must have interested him most, the façade, was scarcely advanced while he held office. He concentrated much of his energy on its planning and, although he did not see his project carried out during his lifetime, we shall find that it had an ineradicable influence on the later history of the façade. Two drawings, the whole façade crowned with high obelisks and accompanied by free-standing campanili (fig. 35), and a large design of half of the façade corresponding exactly to the first drawing (fig. 37), may both be by Pellegrini himself and, if this is correct, they were made for his own files, as we shall see later. Both drawings make it clear that Pellegrini intended to break radically with the Gothic-Seregni tradition and to place a classical façade with immensely powerful Corinthian columns in front of the Gothic cathedral. The fate of Pellegrini's design or designs for the façade was most peculiar. A document of 26 August 1610 informs us that after Pellegrini's death in 1596, his most carefully executed design of the façade had been handed on from one architect to the next and had finally come into the hands of Antonio Maria Corbetta.[14] Nowadays scarcely known, this Corbetta enjoyed some reputation in his day. He was Architect to the Cathedral from 1606 to 1609, and after his dismissal—so the 1610 document inform us—Pellegrini's project could not be found. Corbetta maintained that he had taken it back to the archive from where he got it. Nobody seems to have believed him. The Vicar General summoned him and threatened him with excommunication if he would not return the project. No result. In April 1611 Rome was called upon to act and served him with a summons aimed at recovering the lost project.[15] Whether or not as a result of this action, three years later a torn Pellegrini drawing stretched on blue linen turned up in the archive, and the archivist gave it to a carpenter to make a wooden model from it. Once again, the drawing disappeared mysteriously. Exasperation on all sides.[16] In fact, the original design of Pellegrini's final façade project has never been found again.

The disappearance of Pellegrini's façade design was not just a conjurer's trick. It seems that from the beginning the Fabbrica had turned against him, probably because of the high-handed manner in which the archbishop had settled him in office. However that may be, the fact is that Pellegrini was scarcely allowed to work in peace. To summarize the situation: animosity against Pellegrini first came into the open when in 1569 Martino Bassi submitted a vigorous attack against him to the Deputies of the Fabbrica.[17] This Martino Bassi, though only twenty-seven years old, was not a negligible person. At the time of the attack he was Engineer to the city of Milan and was still at the beginning of a successful career. Perhaps his best-known later work is the dome that he constructed in 1574 over the great centrally built Early Christian church of S. Lorenzo in Milan. Bassi was not concerned with Pellegrini's façade design; he found grave errors at various points of Pellegrini's work in the cathedral, and the Deputies regarded his strictures as sufficiently important to appoint a commission of five experts to investigate Bassi's allegations. As a result of this investigation Pellegrini was handed a questionnaire of twenty-seven points and was also immediately threatened that, if his answers were delayed by more than eight days, appropriate legal steps would be taken.[18] Some of the questions were of a technical nature, others implied all kinds of insinuations about Pellegrini's conduct of business. Pellegrini had his answers ready.[19] Although one can read between the lines that he was bursting with anger, he was courteous, respectful, and patient. He began: "I am benefitting by the belief that you, distinguished, reverend, and admirable gentlemen are seeking explanations regarding some of my actions in the cathedral for the sake of satisfying your conscience, but I hope I will benefit even more by the occasion which you offer me of demonstrating to you, gentlemen, and to the world that I am used to working with reason and not at random. . . ." After this dignified start, he runs through point by point at very great length. Only once or twice one comes across such a turn of phrase as: "It should be obvious even to a mediocre intelligence, etc." In winding up, he lays the cards on the table. I will only quote one sentence: "In case [he says] you would like to gather more information and to have outside opinions in order to be able to assess the matters that have here been discussed, I hope that you will not elect those who never cease persecuting me nor those who distrust me, but men who have confidence in me. . . ." Pellegrini's defense was so convincing and so well phrased that the committee sitting in judgment cleared him unanimously of all accusations and declared Martino Bassi's criticisms to be unfounded. Pellegrini's exoneration was expressed in a legally phrased Latin statement signed by the notary of the Cathedral and by St. Charles Borromeo himself.[20] So, it is clear that St. Charles Borromeo regarded this affair as sufficiently important to necessitate his presence at the meeting and to steer the committee with a firm hand in the direction he wanted.

But now Martino Bassi decided to reinforce his attack with even heavier guns. Barely three years after Pellegrini had been cleared, Bassi published a book entitled (in translation) *Discussion in Matters of Architecture and Perspective with Evaluations by Excellent and Famous Architects.*[21] This little book, that appeared in 1572, was mainly concerned with what Bassi regarded as Pellegrini's faulty rendering of perspective in a relief of the Annunciation that was to be placed above the portal of the north entrance to the cathedral. The story has gained art-historical notoriety and has often been told, for, shortly after his defeat by Pellegrini, Bassi had the nerve to canvass some of the most famous masters, and, strangely enough, he received answers from Palladio, Vignola, Vasari, and the (then well known) Mantuan architect Giovanni Battista Bertani. All four (how else could it have been?) sided with Bassi against Pellegrini. Nevertheless, for the moment Pellegrini seemed firmly installed, though Bassi's latest sally was by no means the end of Pellegrini's troubles. A few years later, in 1582, we hear that the Vicar General absolved him of all accusations made by the Deputies,[22] but despite this verdict renewed accusations were raised early in 1584. Martino Bassi, of all people, was now elected to act as intermediary between the Fabbrica and Pellegrini.[23] Once again, Pellegrini was acquitted of all charges. This happened, however, in March 1585,[24] after Pellegrini had resigned his office as architect of the works. The situation in Milan had changed radically. St. Charles Borromeo had died on 3 November 1584, and, without his mentor, protector, and patron, Pellegrini's disappearance from the scene became inevitable. He accepted Philip II's invitation to come to Spain and help finish the pictorial decoration of the Escorial. He returned home only in 1596. He died in Milan eighty-two days after his arrival. Owing to the dual disaster, St. Charles's death and the departure of the energetic architect, the affairs of the cathedral slackened, until **Cardinal Federico Borromeo** was elected Archbishop of Milan some ten years later and settled in the city in 1601. He immediately showed his determination to continue both the religious and artistic legacy left by his great cousin. But the intervening period of almost two decades had not been entirely barren.

At last Martino Bassi found himself in a position without competitors; in 1587 he was elected to the office of his old enemy and remained architect to the Fabbrica until his death in 1591. He was not satisfied with carrying on what Pellegrini had left unfinished. On 20 December 1590 he urged the Fabbrica to get active on at least one of several major projects. He seemed to have set his mind on the planning of the façade, and the deputies themselves, addressing him in Vitruvian terms, urged him to make a façade design that would not fail to fulfill the demands of eurythmy, symmetry, and decoration. Thus, they clearly expected a classical design. Bassi had not only one ready, but three to choose from, or perhaps even four (figs. 39, 40). On 1 April 1591 Martino Bassi's designs for the façade were sent to Rome so that Pope Gregory XIV, himself a member of the Milanese Sfondrati family, might make his choice.[25] The result seems to have been negative, for on 6 August 1592, i.e., about a year after Bassi's death, the Fabbrica tried to secure new projects for the façade (as the document says) from the most famous architects in Rome, Florence, Venice, and Spain.[26] Spain, at this moment, must have meant Pellegrino Pellegrini. This opens up interesting perspectives, for now three possibilities have to be considered: (1) Pellegrini may not have reacted at all (he was immensely busy in the Escorial); (2) he may have reacted and supplied a new design in addition to the design he had made during his time of office; (3) his design in response to the Fabbrica's new request may in fact have been the first façade design he had ever made.

While Italian scholars have never asked these questions and always took it for granted that Pellegrini's design dated from before his resignation in 1584, a well-informed Austrian art historian, Hans Hoffmann, strongly advocated the third alternative.[27] He felt that the documents spoke a very clear language and that it was really Bassi who in 1590 had first opened up the question of the erection of the façade. This last position cannot be seriously maintained, however, for we must take into account that Vincenzo Seregni designed a façade as early as 1537. Moreover, a certain Tolomeo Rinaldi came out with an elaborate façade project on 17 December 1590, three days before the meeting that gave Bassi the green light (fig. 41).

We know very little about Tolomeo Rinaldi; we do know, however, that he was an opponent of Bassi's, but that nevertheless —in accordance with a well-established Milanese method of procedure— he succeeded Bassi as architect to the church of S. Lorenzo; we have information of some other work of his and also know that he was still alive in 1609. Moreover, there are indications that Bassi knew Rinaldi's project: compare, for instance, the use both architects made of high bases for the order, or the central motif of paired columns flanking the main portal and topped by a segmental pediment that is superimposed on the base of the upper tier. Finally, there are distinct links between Bassi's project (fig. 40) and Pellegrini's (fig. 35): one has only to remark the high obelisks placed on top of the lower tier; they presuppose Bassi's knowledge of Pellegrini's design. So we have to conclude that Pellegrini had indeed made a façade design before his abdication. I am, on the other hand, most doubtful about any action having been undertaken by him in this matter in 1592 from his Spanish abode.

Even without taking the story further, we can conclude that one of the critical moments in the affairs of the façade was the time around 1580, when Pellegrini's project should be dated. We have seen that such Renaissance masters as Leonardo, Bramante, and Vincenzo Seregni (to whom others could be added) favored Gothic or quasi-Gothic solutions, and that it was only Pellegrini who, close to the end of the sixteenth century, turned decisively to devising projects in a contemporary rather than a historic style. Many (including Bassi and Rinaldi) followed him, and for half a century Pellegrini's classical approach was accepted as paradigmatic. In the next chapter, we will therefore have to consider his project more thoroughly and carry the story forward to the moment when a renewed volte-face, a renewed turn toward Gothic solutions, caused Pellegrini's project to tumble.

CHAPTER II

The Façade of
Milan Cathedral:
Classic Solutions and
Gothic Volte-face

BEFORE RETURNING to the projects for the façade of Milan Cathedral by Pellegrino Pellegrini and his immediate followers, I want to present some factual material and also to indicate the strategy of the present chapter. This seems to me necessary since I will be dealing with a fair amount of miscellaneous material and have also to mention many names scarcely known even to professional art historians. As an old classroom performer I will therefore use a classroom technique that may be helpful in finding a way through a tangle of detail.

First let us consider a list of the cathedral architects from the mid-sixteenth to the early years of the nineteenth century (see p. 186). On this list there are twenty-four names. The first three (Seregni, Pellegrini, and Bassi) we have encountered, and I had mentioned Corbetta, who had lost, stolen, or hidden Pellegrini's façade project. Some of the remaining twenty names (such as Trezzi, the Bisnati, father and son, the three members of the Quadrio family, and Andrea Biffi) are only of marginal interest in our context. Three seventeenth-century cathedral architects made designs for the façade which survive, namely Francesco Maria Ricchino, Fabio Mangone, and Carlo Buzzi; of these Ricchino and Buzzi will require our most careful attention. Among the eighteenth-century cathedral architects, Giulio Galliori's and Soave's designs will engage us and finally also the designs by Pollak and Amati, which take us to the façade we see today.

Now some of the most interesting façade designs were made by outsiders, i.e., architects not officially appointed to the cathedral, and the controversies that ensued came also to a considerable extent from outside experts called in by the Fabbrica. I am therefore supplementing the list of cathedral architects by a chart of façade projects in chronological sequence (see p. 187). This list—though longer than that of the cathedral architects—is far from complete, but it contains, at least, the names of all those architects who were paid for designs. We have encountered already the first names on this list, those of Seregni, Pellegrini, Rinaldi, Bassi, Ricchino. We have projects (with very few exceptions now in the Ambrosiana and the Castello Sforzesco in Milan) by all those architects whose names are underlined. The identification of their drawings is usually possible because of an autograph or contemporary inscriptions.

Going down the list, we see that Onorio Longhi's two projects (for which he was paid) are lost or not yet known. Longhi was a fairly distinguished architect who came from Lombardy, but had made his name in Rome, where he died in 1619. Then follows a series of identifiable drawings and, apart from the names of the cathedral architects Ricchino, Mangone, Buzzi, you find two names here (Gerolamo da Sesto De Capitaneis and Francesco Castelli) about whom more will be said later. Among the next group of four architects whose projects are unknown there are two names of art-historical nonentities (Pagani and Villa), while Juvarra, the Piedmontese court architect, was of course one of the greatest eighteenth-century architects and Francesco Croce, a Milanese celebrity, promoter of an elegant late eighteenth-century manner, was cathedral architect and built, during his tenure of office, the spire over the *Tiburio* (on which I commented in the previous chapter). Among the following group of identified designs there appear two great outsiders, Vanvitelli and Vittone; of the others Merlo had a local reputation (and has recently even been deemed worthy of a long monograph by M. L. Cratti Perer, Milan, 1966) but Vertemate Cotognola and Riccardi are practically unknown magnitudes.

Although we have records of many discussions following the submission of façade projects, there occurred three major controversies which I have noted on the list of façade designers: one after Ricchino's 1606 project, the second after Castelli's project of 1648, and the third following Vanvitelli's of 1745. For our purposes the controversy after 1648 is the most interesting one and will be discussed at some length.

Finally, I have subdivided my list into five sections—and this for two reasons. Looking at the sections simply as chronological statements, you will notice that the planning of the façade did not engage the Fabbrica uninterruptedly through more than 250 years. Leaving Seregni aside, there was a first bout of activity during approximately the decade from 1580 to 1590. After an interval there was new assiduous planning between 1603 and 1610. Then a pause, scarcely broken, of more than three decades, followed by a string of projects and many discussions between 1642 and 1656. Then once again a gap, this time a long one of seventy-seven years. Between 1733 and 1746 the façade seemed to become an urgent problem; but once again the planning fever subsided. With the return to active planning in the final years of the eighteenth century, the matter remained alive until a project was realized through Napoleon's dictatorial intervention.

By concentrating on these five fairly isolated periods of planning, I not only intended to bring some chronological order into this remarkable enterprise, but had a more interesting point in mind. We can discern revealing stylistic changes from period to period. The projects made during the first two periods are, broadly speaking, classical—"Roman," as they were called at the time. The planners of the third period (toward the middle of the seventeenth century) turned away from classical designs, either back to Gothic or to what they called mixed designs. During the fourth period the projects were also Gothic, but it was perhaps a more imaginative, more fanciful Gothic manner than that of the third stage. The Gothic projects of the fifth phase take on a sober neo-Gothic character, and it is not without interest to note that these authors consciously sought and found inspiration in the mid-seventeenth-century Gothic designs.

It is now time to return once more to Pellegrini's "Roman" design. "Roman" here is, of course, a generic term indicating that all the elements of the design—the orders, the shape and frames of doors and windows, the obelisks and decorative features—are of classical derivation, but at the time this design was made (about 1580) there was no similar church façade in Rome, nor were there any at a later

date. The engraving of 1646 which is inscribed "Pellegrinus invenit"
(fig. 36) fully agrees with the drawings discussed in the previous
chapter. Thus we can be pretty certain that this is Pellegrini's final
design, particularly since the engraving was made at the request of
the Fabbrica in order to present a correct idea of Pellegrini's project.
The principal motif of the façade is the row of giant columns, over
sixty feet in height, with shafts that were each planned to be of one
enormous piece of marble; this row of columns was meant to be
freestanding, but as the plan shows, each column was to be linked to
a half-column behind it, set into the wall of the façade. In Pellegrini's
design the columns have a distinctly vertical tendency: they carry
projecting pieces of entablature crowned by figures and obelisks. This
splendid procession of columns is as un-Roman as the overrich
decoration with figures and small-size reliefs. When such mighty
columns appear a little later in Rome (incidentally, not without
Lombard influence) they are—as in the façade of S. Peter's—firmly
attached to the wall and appear to be structural rather than decorative
members (fig. 43).

It would be a mistake to believe that Pellegrini's façade was
designed without regard to the Gothic structure behind it. On the
contrary, the peculiar organization of the columns—paired at the
corners and in the center framing the main door and single ones
between the side doors (a sequence that lacks rhythmic deployment
or any kind of dynamic movement)—is determined by the plan of
the church. This is immediately evident if one looks at an old plan
with Pellegrini's façade (fig. 38) (there are strong indications that
this plan came from Pellegrini's studio): the columns respond to the
massive pieces of wall at the corners and to the interior rows of piers,
and it is certainly not by chance that the clear width between the two
pairs of columns in the center is that of half of the nave. It is likely
that the six tall, elegant obelisks were chosen as topping decorations
because they may be regarded as classical counterparts to the tapering
pinnacles of the Gothic structure. We also know that Pellegrini had
the intention of linking the Gothic and Roman parts, for he wanted
to carry the cornice of the façade around the entire church; he planned
a leaden roof and wanted to abolish all German finials.[1] Despite such
ideas Pellegrini was not entirely out of sympathy with the Gothic
style. When he was asked for his advice regarding S. Petronio at
Bologna, he was not opposed to a Gothic façade if the older Gothic
parts had to be preserved, and he supported his view with the words:
"It would please me if one would follow as far as possible the precepts

of that manner, for they are more reasonable than people believe. . . ."[2] In a sense, we are back to Vasari's ambiguous position toward the Gothic style, although one has to state that Pellegrini was less biased than his great contemporary and that he was able to see reason—and that implies order—where Vasari negatively found only confusion and disorder. Pellegrini preferred, of course, a Roman to a Gothic façade, but when he was advising the Bolognese and when he was planning for Milan Cathedral the concept of conformity, of stylistic unity, was constantly on his mind.

In spite of the opposition to Pellegrini during his tenure of office and the later continuous attempts to rid the Fabbrica of his project, some decisive action was taken. In August 1583—while he was still in office—a contract was signed for the construction of the foundations of the main portal of the façade.[3] By January 1602 the foundations of the façade had progressed so far that the deputies had to get permission to pull down a projecting part of the Ducal Palace which jutted out into the southwest corner of the area of the new façade.[4] Many sixteenth- and seventeenth-century plans give a clear idea of this situation (fig. 11).

In April 1609 a definite decision was taken to carry out the rest of Pellegrini's project, but some modifications were requested regarding the upper tier.[5] It was not long after this decision that Corbetta spirited away the project in question. But this did not seriously interfere with the work. Let me immediately give additional information about the progress made in the execution of Pellegrini's façade design. In mid-1616 negotiations began about the marble for the columns, the most vexing problem offered by this project.[6] In April 1618 the first of the huge column shafts was secured in the quarry at Baveno on Lago Maggiore. During the transport the shaft broke into three pieces and it is therefore not astonishing that the matter rested for some time—to be exact, for almost seven years. But early in 1625 a powerful commission of experts under the Archbishop was summoned in order to investigate the problem of the columns.[7] Over a year later Ricchino, who was a member of the Commission, declared that he would be able to undertake the safe transport of the columns for two thousand scudi each.[8] This was a great deal of money (Ricchino's annual salary as Cathedral Architect was only two hundred scudi). In 1629 Ricchino's transport proposition was still being discussed.

The doors presented lesser problems. Great care was taken to guarantee precise and successful execution. Thus in November 1628 a carpenter was paid for wooden models of the outside as well as the inside of the main portal.[9] In June 1631 a contract was signed for the ornaments of one of the side doors, and in September 1634 for those of one of the windows over a side door.[10] At this time (3 August) one side door was completed, a second one was almost finished, and the others were far advanced (fig. 18). Whereas the side doors almost correspond to those of the engraving, the windows do not. Nor do the details of the main door, such as the shape of the pediment. It is worth noting that the painter Cerano had a hand in this part of the building. One of the great figures among Milanese painters at the beginning of the seventeenth century, Cerano was appointed head of the cathedral workshop of sculpture in 1629 and in this capacity he designed much of the sculptural decorations of the portal. An architectural drawing of the central portal area, signed by him, has even survived in the Ambrosiana. It may have been executed in preparation of the wooden model of 1628, but it is also still somewhat removed from the final treatment of the door pediment and the inset panel for sculpture.

At this point I would like to discuss two old views of the façade, one dating from 1650 (fig. 17), the other from 1735 (fig. 19). Both views demonstrate (the later one in considerable detail) how far the execution of Pellegrini's façade had progressed. We see that work came to a halt after the five portals and the windows above the northern side portals had practically been finished. It is obvious that no later architect could plan without taking into consideration the parts that were standing. This fact we will have to keep in mind. So, Pellegrini will always make his presence known, to the very end of this story. But I have to call attention to one other feature. Disregarding for the moment the half-finished elements framing the main portal, we notice giant paired pilasters at the corner and a single pilaster between the side doors; these pilasters rise directly from the ground and are still without capitals. According to the various plans we have studied there should have been half-columns here. But there is in existence another set of designs, all coming from Ricchino, which, in the ground plan, show pilasters instead of half-columns in these positions. The key piece is a large engraving (signed by Ricchino) dated 1635, i.e., during Ricchino's tenure of office, which illustrates alternative projects (fig. 44): the left half is inscribed below: "Design of the Cathedral of Milan with the lower tier according to Pellegrini's project" and the right side bears the inscription: "New Design of the façade of the Cathedral according to the project of the Architect

Ricchino. Engineer of the Reverend Fabbrica." Ricchino does not claim to follow Pellegrini's design in the upper tier (see fig. 36). It seems that he had in mind the Fabbrica verdict of 1609 according to which Pellegrini's upper tier needed revision.[11] (This was a verdict, by the way, that surely reflected older criticism.) In this area Ricchino took over some Pellegrini elements, such as the high attic with reliefs set into it and the shape of the central window, but the changes he devised are more significant. The entire tier has been considerably heightened and broadened, the columns have assumed greater weight; the small-scale double niches one above the other, for which there was space between the paired columns, have been transformed, as it were, into a large niche, filling the space of a new side bay next to the central bay. There are many other changes: let me only mention that instead of the simple concave buttress supporting the upper tier one finds an elaborate scroll and that the figures are no longer placed in front of the attic, but above it. On the right-hand side, which Ricchino claims for himself, there appear a number of interesting alterations, which on the whole tend to give the design a more baroque character, such as the enlargement of the central window and the pulling together of the individual pedestals with statues silhouetted against the sky by the introduction of a coherent balustrade.

These new elements introduced by Ricchino were definitely influenced by impressions he had received much earlier during a stay in Rome of some duration in the first years of the seventeenth century.[12] He then saw Maderno's S. Susanna practically finished and was apparently very impressed (fig. 42). Such features as the buttresses ending in large scrolls, the continuous balustrade on top and the balustrades in front of the windows, as well as the unbroken segmental pediment over the central door and the unbroken triangular pediment over the paired columns of the central bay, are derived from Maderno. Since Ricchino incorporated some of these new features also in the portion of the design he labelled as being by Pellegrini, I have come to the conclusion that the changeover from half-columns to pilasters along the wall was also Ricchino's. He himself was so much involved in the problems of quarrying and transporting the columns that he must have felt the situation would be somewhat eased by relinquishing the plan to use half-columns in addition to the full columns.

It is not without interest that a preparatory drawing for the engraving, also signed by Ricchino, has survived (fig. 45). In relation to the engraving it is reversed as it should be, but it is unfinished, for at the last moment, it seems, Ricchino decided to introduce some minor changes. Finally, there is in existence a sheet that was concocted from a correct pull of the left-hand side of the engraving and a reversed pull of the same design on the right—the whole producing what purports to be a complete view of Pellegrini's design, but is, in reality, as we have seen, Ricchino's reinterpretation of it, mainly in the vastly changed upper tier (fig. 46). The same procedure was followed in the design which Ricchino described as his own: an engraving of the entire façade was produced, the two sides of which are mirror images of each other (fig. 47). The advantage of this method consists in offering the beholder a complete rather than a fragmentary image of the design. A point that is important and here clearly visible is that Ricchino intended to separate the lower from the upper tier by the rigid barrier of an unbroken entablature; this is, of course, in sharpest contrast with the verticalism and the interlocking of the two tiers planned by Pellegrini. It seems that by isolating the row of columns Ricchino wanted to emphasize their power, grandeur, and cohesion. And, in fact, the columns in the Ricchino project appear more effective than in the project of their originator. As we have seen, Ricchino published the material we have just examined in 1635. In this year he requested, and was granted, an increase in salary as Architect to the Cathedral as compensation for his extraordinary work, in particular in connection with the new designs of the façade. Thus we are entitled to conclude that we have before us the project Ricchino recommended for execution in 1635.

Now Ricchino was surely the most gifted and most resourceful Milanese architect of the first half, if not of the entire seventeenth century, and in the course of more than three decades he turned again and again to the façade of the cathedral and suggested ever-new projects. They are linked by being variations of the Roman manner; but, although they show certain common idiosyncrasies of style, they are still so different that without the signatures one would hesitate to ascribe them all to the same hand.

On my chart (p. 187) I have listed other documented designs by Ricchino of 1603, 1606, and 1610. A highly finished design which contains two alternative projects—immediately revealed by the different types of columns left and right—can be associated (and I believe, has often been associated) with the 1603 project (fig. 48). As the inscription in the cartouche on the top left informs us, the young architect, who in 1603 was only nineteen years old, had made this design as an offering of thanks to his patron, Cardinal Federico Borromeo, after his return from Rome. The impact Rome had made upon Ricchino is apparent in his use of the corkscrew columns and the columns decorated with the vine leaves which he had seen in S. Peter's. Without discussing this project in any detail, I would like only to point out that one easily discovers in it many recollections of Pellegrini as well as some restless, erratic features of Mannerist derivation. But what is more interesting is that the plan of the façade is not yet tied to Pellegrini's: by 1603, the foundations were not yet finished and the situation was still fluid (see fig. 36). So Ricchino was able to propose a front in two planes (the outside bays are recessed) and with columns set against segmental cavities in the wall.

Let me recall that the decision to build Pellegrini's façade was only taken in 1609; thus in 1606 one could still be daring and play about with quite different solutions. Ricchino's project of that year (fig. 49) had grown more massive and more solid; the columns of the main story have been reduced in height and the second tier has gained in importance. The principal point of this plan, however, is its deployment in three planes; one bay is in a different layer from the next, the wall is in motion, and there is a notable emphasis on the center bay. These were all ideas Ricchino may have carried away from Rome, although the use of such an array of freestanding columns in a church façade did not occur in Rome until the mid-century.

At this point I would like to interpolate the project of the practically unknown Gerolamo da Sesto De Capitaneis, dating from 1608 (fig. 53) and clearly dependent on Ricchino's project of 1606. There is here a further concentration toward the center: we now find a cluster of three columns on each side of the central portal; certain features hark back to Pellegrini, but there are obvious weaknesses in this work on which we hardly need to spend time. One element, however, has to be mentioned, the lower order is not firmly planted on the ground, but rises from high pedestals.

Ricchino himself was converted to this solution in two strange projects which may date from 1610 (figs. 50, 51). Both projects show campanili connected with the façade—square towers projecting from the straight wall: the idea quite distinctly goes back to Seregni's proposals of over seventy years before (fig. 32). Both projects accept the by-now axiomatic Pellegrini front with an aligned row of free-standing columns, and both pick up a great many older details. The one project (fig. 51), for instance, follows fairly closely Pellegrini's organization of the central bay with a niche for the statue of the Virgin placed into the large broken pediment (fig. 35). The window above, the paired columns with niches between them, the obelisks—all this and much more has a clear Pellegrinian pedigree. A flap of paper can be turned down to cover the second tier. It shows how this tier could be expanded and modernized without interfering with the basic design (fig. 52). This second project (fig. 35) shows two alternatives, mainly different elaborations of the second tier; but there are also important differences below: the right-hand side, for instance, shows Pellegrini's half-columns set against the wall. We need not go into further details. Let me only mention that the Palladian window in the upper tier of the left-hand design stems directly from Bassi's project of 1590-91 (fig. 39 or 40), and there are other, perhaps less obvious, connections with Bassi. In any case, he too had chosen high pedestals for his order. So it would seem that at this stage Ricchino tried to impress the Fabbrica by dishing up traditional fare rather than his own bolder inventions, and this is my main reason for suggesting the date 1610 for these designs: they look like frantic attempts to do something old-fashioned and super-Pellegrinesque in order to induce the Fabbrica to reverse their 1609 decisions in favor of himself, Ricchino. Compared with such designs, his project of 1635 (fig. 47) strikes one as the mature statement of a man conscious of carrying the responsibility of office and who must have felt that his privileged position would help gain acceptance of a grand balanced design that summed up the essence of Pellegrini's work and surpassed it.

Despite the variety of Ricchino's façade designs, we have to admit that he was the seventeenth-century standard-bearer of Pellegrini's Roman solution. There are more Ricchino drawings for the façade in Milan, but they would scarcely add to what we have learned. There are also a number of projects in existence by other architects of this period who could only think in terms of the Pellegrini-Ricchino designs. The best among these projects is Fabio Mangone's, published in 1642, thirteen years after its author's death (fig. 56). This project dates possibly from between 1617 and 1629, the period of Mangone's tenure of office as cathedral architect, but it may, of course, date earlier, perhaps around 1610, when the façade was much discussed. Next to Ricchino, Mangone was the strongest Milanese architect in the second and third decades of the seventeenth century. His severe design for the façade, perhaps the most Roman that was ever created, shows his real strength: characteristically, in 1620 Cardinal Federico Borromeo appointed him Professor of Architecture at the newly formed Accademia Ambrosiana.

Mangone's teacher, Alessandro Bisnati (Cathedral Architect from 1609 to 1617) and his son Giovan Paolo Bisnati (Cathedral Architect from 1617 to 1625 next to and under Mangone) also made Roman designs, and Giovan Paolo specifically studied the flank of his façade in relation to the side of the cathedral (fig. 54). As others before him, he was concerned with the problem of aligning the horizontal breaks of the façade with those of the Gothic building.

I would like to conclude this matter by discussing briefly four more Roman designs of unequal quality, all of them in search of an author. Three of them must be dated in the early years of the seventeenth century and demonstrate with what obsession the Pellegrini-Ricchino concept was recapitulated ad absurdum. These designs have also in common that they show a reorganization of the paired columns in an attempt to produce an unbroken sequence. The first drawing takes up Ricchino's corkscrew-column project of 1603, but places the order on high pedestals: obviously drawn by an architect with a penchant for decorative motifs (fig. 55). No less obsessed was the author of the next design (fig. 57), who was probably an amateur. The obesity of his columns led to underdeveloped spaces between them, while his eccentric decorative features, above all the small four-tiered transformations of obelisks, were apparently invented to tie up with the Gothic detail. The next two drawings were made by architects of some standing. First (fig. 58), one which has been attributed to Lelio Buzzi, who was Acting Architect to the Cathedral from 1591 to 1603 but never received a full appointment, and also to Lorenzo Binago, a Barnabite, the architect of S. Alessandro in Milan; he—it is known—was one of those who responded to the Fabbrica's invitation of 1592;[13] but I doubt that a highly skillful architect like Binago would have invented the awkward wall strips with niches in the main tier.

The last drawing of this series may well belong to the eighteenth century (fig. 59). It represents a kind of Pellegrini design stripped of all incidentals; it is beautifully cohesive and shows a steady sequence of paired columns which are carried over into the second tier and the towers. In this project the façade looks like a base for the exceedingly high towers—a typically eighteenth-century idea. Its towers, if built, would have been about three hundred feet tall.

Before taking leave of Pellegrini-Ricchino I wish to comment briefly on the first of the three controversies I had already mentioned. After Ricchino had submitted his 1606 project (fig. 49), the architect, Pietro Antonio Barca—who was a member of the Milanese College of Engineers and Architects from 1577 onward and held the office of engineer to the city of Milan, a man of considerable distinction and

one who enjoyed disputations more than anything else—sent a memorandum to the deputies that begins by praising the cathedral and
pointing out how much more marvelous it would have been had it
been erected in the Roman rather than the German manner.[14] But
the façade, the most noble part of the structure, had to outshine the
German work. He then recorded that back in December of 1603
the Fabbrica had called upon three experts, himself among them, in
order to discuss Pellegrini's project. Pellegrini had planned his columns without pedestals (fig. 36) and this, the commission declared,
was demonstrably a grave mistake. Now, four years after the event,
Barca was giving them all the reasons why columns ought to stand
on pedestals. His arguments are manifold, but an important point
for him, as for all architects dedicated to the classical manner, are
precedents; he therefore gives a long list of important buildings in
Rome, Milan, and elsewhere all showing classical order on pedestals.

In this long document of August 1607 Barca never mentioned
the name Ricchino, but everyone knew, of course, against whom the
barbs of his attack were directed. And so Ricchino answered.[15] His
defense starts with the remark that the ancients never placed pedestals under their columns. He rises in defense of Pellegrini—which
means also of himself—and submits some well-argued points. For
instance, he explains that if one uses pedestals one has to diminish the
size of the columns themselves and consequently that of all the other
members of the façade also and this would be fatal in the case of a
building of the dimensions of Milan Cathedral.

Ricchino's defense is brief and not particularly detailed. The
slaughtering of Barca he seems to have left to one of his friends who
submitted an anti-Barca missive of about three thousand words in
which all the points Barca had made are laboriously refuted.[16] To
this Barca answered in a "Counterattack to an Anonymous Attack."
One thing is strange about this controversy. Ricchino, the champion
of giant columns without pedestals, yielded—as we have seen—during
a brief period to the propedestal party and showed that he could
handle this problem too (figs. 50, 51). I doubt that he made his
elaborate drawings of a façade with columns on pedestals simply to
demonstrate that such designs were not workable. It is even more
puzzling that there exists an old tradition according to which Pellegrini left two projects, one with, and the other without pedestals to
the orders. This tradition goes back to a rare collection of material on
the façade published in Milan about 1656 with the title "Per la facciata
del Duomo." To be sure, Pellegrini did not object to the use of

pedestals under columns. The church of S. Fedele in Milan begun by him in 1569, as well as other buildings of his, prove it. Nevertheless, there is no indication in documents or drawings that he ever considered pedestals for the façade of Milan Cathedral and until such evidence appears, I prefer to trust Ricchino's unambiguous statement made in 1607.

Ricchino had begun serving the Fabbrica in 1603; in 1605 he was appointed "capomastro della Fabbrica del Duomo."[17] As such he had an important function, perhaps comparable to that of a clerk of the works. He was then twenty-one years old and had moved into this position through the support of his lifelong patron, Cardinal Federico Borromeo, who did for him what St. Charles Borromeo had done for Pellegrini. So from 1605 on Ricchino was for many years the most stable figure in the architectural affairs of the Fabbrica. In 1631, when, at the age of forty-seven, he became Architect to the Fabbrica,[18] he was better equipped than anyone before him to fill this difficult office. In the same year, 1631, Ricchino's patron, Cardinal Federico, died and soon thereafter Ricchino had to face problems similar to those of Pellegrini half a century before: in mid-July 1638 he was summarily dismissed and his presence at the Fabbrica was strictly forbidden.[19] He immediately requested to know the reasons for his dismissal so that he would be able to exonerate himself. The matter dragged on for almost a year, Ricchino asking for a written statement that during his service at the Fabbrica he had not disgraced himself either by objectionable or fraudulent practices.[20] Whatever the true reasons for his dismissal were, the men responsible for the Fabbrica had decided to steer an entirely new course. They appointed Carlo Buzzi as Architect to the Cathedral;[21] he was the son of Lelio, whom I had mentioned as Acting Architect from 1591 to 1603. Carlo stayed in office for fully twenty years, to his death in 1658, and during these years revolutionary steps regarding the façade were taken. We have no records of Buzzi's views on the façade at the moment of his stepping into Ricchino's shoes; but it is a fair guess that he had made his ideas known. So far as I am aware there is no major building by him before his appointment, but he himself said that he had served the cathedral from 1623 onward. His known work ties in with the Milanese Renaissance and Mannerist tradition; his façade of the Palazzo delle Scuole Palatine of 1645, for instance, is more or less copied from Seregni's and Alessi's nearby Palazzo dei Giureconsulti, dating from the 1560s. Regarding the cathedral façade, however, Buzzi intended to break with the Roman manner. Three Gothic projects by his hand are known, of which two are identical except that one has towers and the other does not (figs. 61, 62). These are traditionally dated in 1645, i.e., seven years after he had become Cathedral Architect; the third, divergent in a few important respects, definitely dates from 1653 (fig. 60).

I am convinced that Buzzi made, or at least planned, his first two designs (figs. 61, 62) much earlier than 1645—I like to think that his ideas were known in 1638 when he was elected cathedral architect. When, in August 1645, his project was before the deputies, they were fully aware of its importance, for they deferred discussing it to a plenary meeting of the Cathedral Chapter.[22] Meanwhile they asked Buzzi for a written report stating his reasons why the old projects should be abandoned. Four days later the report was in the hands of the deputies,[23] and it is therefore most likely that Buzzi had had all his arguments ready for some time. It was decided that both the new project and the report should be published. It was further resolved that the three projects under consideration, Pellegrini's, Ricchino's, and Buzzi's, should be engraved, undoubtedly in order to give each deputy a chance of comparing in his own time the pros and cons of each design.

By February 1646 Buzzi's (figs. 61, 62), Pellegrini's (fig. 36), and Ricchino's (figs. 44, 47) projects had been engraved and printed. As regards Buzzi's the Chapter decided that one half of it should be carried out as a wooden model.[24] Buzzi presented the engraving of his project at a meeting in December 1646 and on this occasion it was reiterated that this was a matter of such momentous importance that a decision should be deferred to a plenary meeting.[25] From then on the affair developed a little more rapidly. A few days after the December meeting Buzzi addressed a letter[26] to the chapter in which he said he had followed their commands and had submitted a design for the façade in correspondence with the structure (or let us say: style) of the cathedral. For reasons known to the deputies he had, however, preserved the parts that had already been built. This letter was meant to prepare the members for the plenary session that took place on the last day of January 1647, on which occasion Buzzi's report was read. It began (I contract somewhat):

> This illustrious Chapter has asked me to make a new design of the façade the engraving of which is appended. This design is a compound of Roman and Gothic architecture [è composto d'architettura mista di romana e di gotica] for reasons I am herewith stating. In

the first place I have taken care that the part executed in the Roman manner and the portion that remains to be done shall be compatible.[27]

The old axiom was very much on Buzzi's mind. The remaining points, many of them of a practical nature, can be stated briefly: The "Roman" project would be too high (fig. 36); it would hide the upper portion of the cathedral, which is its most beautiful and most ornate part. (This, surely, signals a new attitude: the forest of pinnacles, to earlier generations an abomination, was now appreciated as aesthetically most satisfactory). Also, the central window of the Roman project would be too high, for it would be partly above the vault of the nave: the aisles adjoining the nave would not have sufficient light, for windows, where he himself had placed them, could not be placed in a Roman design because they would interfere with the horizontal entablature, a sine qua non of the Roman manner. A Gothic design would automatically solve the perplexing problem of the ten giant column shafts.[28] Not only this, but many other difficulties could be avoided by building the façade in conformity with the rest of the cathedral. Finally, he says, architecturally speaking, there is no doubt at all that the new design goes better with the body of the church. Moreover, one has to keep in mind that in the Gothic interior of the cathedral there are many works executed in the Roman manner, such as the altars, the enclosure in the choir, the crypt, the high altar, the ornament of the organs, the baptistery, and so forth (by the way, all these works enumerated by Buzzi were designed by Pellegrini) and none of these features, he carries on, are repugnant. A similar mixture of styles in the façade is justified and acceptable, especially in view of the necessity to use what has been built and the problems which are inherent in the Roman design and to which he, Buzzi, has referred at length.

All this is immensely interesting and revealing: it must be called a real breakthrough. The old problem of uniformity takes on a new meaning, for Buzzi is entirely unprejudiced and can even apply the epithet "beautiful" to the *maniera tedesca* without fear of betraying principles. He has an entirely open mind toward both styles and can see and appreciate them side by side. Indeed, the so-called mixed style he advocates is not just a makeshift solution that offered itself in a bottleneck situation, but—he makes it quite clear—there is no reason why it should not be acceptable and even satisfactory. The nineteenth century was less open-minded, as we shall see shortly.

Buzzi had propagated his case most effectively, as two further developments go to show. Early in 1653 he came out with a project that was more radical (fig. 60): it contained significant emendations of the earlier project, although the overall conception remained the same. When he conceived the first project, he felt he had to continue the windows in the Roman manner. The two windows of the third tier giving light to the vault of the aisles as well as the windows above the main portal were his. But now, true to his own advocacy of mixed styles, he did the logical thing: he redesigned the two side windows as Gothic windows and replaced the two central windows by an enormously high Gothic one. This project was now accepted for execution. How seriously it was then taken is demonstrated by the fact that the execution of the twin pilaster strips over pedestals framing the central portal was immediately taken in hand. The engraving of 1735 reveals that they never got beyond the height of the door (fig. 19). But there they were, and the combination of Pellegrini's doors and windows with Ricchino's classical wall pilasters and Buzzi's Gothic pilaster strips on pedestals tied the hands of every later architect.

Buzzi's 1653 project was the outcome of a fight for survival. His first Gothic design must have made an immense impression even outside the immediate circle of the Fabbrica. It encouraged a young man, Francesco Castelli (1615–1692), to try his hand at a design. He, it must be said, had earlier connections with the Fabbrica, for it was he who had prepared the design for the 1646 engraving of Pellegrini's project (fig. 36). He started as a student of perspective and painting and I believe his first architectural works date from about 1660. In 1648, when he sent his design to the Fabbrica, he was thirty-three years old (fig. 64). I may perhaps dub his design a super-Buzzi. Clearly, he tried to take the wind out of the Cathedral Architect's sails. The first impression is that of a rather uncontrolled, mad affair. Who would have believed that this sort of design was possible in the mid-seventeenth century? Well, in actual fact, it is a very shrewd project and its author was an excellent promoter. It caused a greater stir than any other project of the façade and almost toppled Buzzi. The strange story of Francesco Castelli is told in chapter three.

CHAPTER **III**

The Façade of
Milan Cathedral:
Gothic Designs

A GREAT DEAL about Castelli (fig. 64) must still be buried in the Milanese archives. But, mainly owing to recent research,[1] he is beginning to take on a distinct physiognomy. Carlo Buzzi, the Cathedral Architect, died on or shortly before 26 September 1658. A week later, at their meeting of 3 October, the Deputies decided to make a new appointment. On that day they had before them a long letter by Castelli formally applying with a great deal of eloquence for the coveted job.[2] His opponents, he said, declared that he was a mere student and painter of perspective and not an architect. Before the Deputies knew what had happened, he had proved to them most skillfully that perspective and architecture were interdependent disciplines. For his arguments he ransacked Renaissance art theory. They must have been impressed by his letter, but at the same time they seem to have been convinced that they needed a less colorful person and appointed Buzzi's solidly trained pupil Gerolamo Quadrio to the office.[3] Some years later Castelli wrote a treatise on geometry entitled (in translation) "Treatise on Practical Geometry according to the Doctrines of Euclid, Albrecht Dürer and Cosimo Bartoli written by the Architect Francesco Castelli for the Instruction of the Milanese Academy."[4] The work remained unfinished and was never published, probably because the professorship of architecture at the Academy, at which Castelli was aiming, was permanently suspended in 1669. But what exists of the treatise shows that Castelli was a man of considerable erudition who was capable of a clear, logical, and concise presentation of his material.

Let us look at the sequence of events. On 14 May 1648 we hear that the Chapter resolved to inspect "a project for the façade made by an architect,"[5] who was, in fact, Castelli. The matter was serious enough to call in expert opinion. Two experts were close at hand and were asked to write reports. They were Ricchino, whose relation to the Fabbrica was rather strained after his dismissal from office ten years before, and Carlo Buzzi, the Cathedral Architect in office, whose own project was under close, favorable consideration.[6] The first round ended with the decision of the chapter to have these memoranda printed so that everyone would have a chance to form his own opinion. The second round began late in 1651 when Castelli, by order of the Fabbrica, made a second design which he had engraved (fig. 67).[7] Again by commission of the Chapter, he executed half of this design as a wooden model late in 1652. On the basis of the engraved design new expert opinion was sought. There was a third round or rather an aftermath to the experts' memoranda in 1656. And after this—silence.

Some of the memoranda and Castelli's reaction to them are of great interest and I shall try to convey some of the flavor of the controversy. But before doing this, let us take a dispassionate look at Castelli's design. I would like to make eight brief points: (1) Like Buzzi (fig. 61), Castelli preserved the Roman portion of the façade that had been executed, but found an ingenious method of subduing it: he pushed it back into a shaded area, as it were, by placing a shallow Gothic portico in front of it. (2) The columns of the portico are given bases and capitals corresponding to those of the piers inside the cathedral (fig. 7), but the shafts have screwlike spiral threads with decorations along the grooves in the manner of the twelfth-century Roman Cosmati. The columns are linked by Gothic arches of varying width and height. (3) Again, corresponding to the interior, the columns carry half-columns apparently accompanied by column-ettes and above them rests a cornice that forms a horizontal barrier across the façade. (4) Above the cornice is a gallery with a balustrade consisting of Gothic pyramidal balusters which take up a crowning motif of the Gothic Cathedral (fig. 8). The sequence of these balusters is interrupted at certain intervals by posts continuing the order under-neath. (5) The second tier basically repeats the organization of the portico front underneath, but not in the same plane, for the architectural features are attached to the wall of the cathedral: a relatively low order of half-columns with unusual ornamental designs on the shafts are topped, as below, by Gothic arches and relatively simple compound pilasters. (6) The central window and the large, relief-filled panels of the side bays continue the Roman design of doors and windows underneath and are actually borrowed directly from Ricchino's design (fig. 47). (7) Finally, the cornice has a baroque, Borrominesque swing, but is in reality indebted to the silhouette of the medieval façade of the old cathedral S. Maria Maggiore, a façade that was then still standing inside the nave of the new cathedral (fig. 16). Castelli's façade is crowned by a continuous sequence of the kind of pyramidal decoration which we have encountered already and by pinnacles placed above the orders. (8) It might be added that some other motifs are worth noting such as the large scrolls at the sides of the upper tier; they belong to the Renaissance repertory, but have assumed here a strange character by virtue of their decoration with Gothic crockets.

Largely owing to this kind of rethinking and reinterpreting of classical forms, Castelli's project must have appealed enormously to contemporaries. One of them, Lucio Binago, probably expressed what many felt.[8] Castelli, he wrote, makes himself the propagator of a *new* Gothic manner which conforms with Roman architecture, while the *ancient* Gothic manner revived by Buzzi is entirely incompatible with the Roman portions of the façade. At first this may be difficult for us to follow, but upon consideration it implies a support of nonconformity against orthodoxy. Obviously, we will have a good deal to learn if we want to understand the approach of some or many seventeenth-century people to Buzzi's and Castelli's Gothic, and I hope it is now clear that Castelli's was a very well considered and entirely serious project.

We will get more into the spirit of the controversy by following the written discussion. Attack and counterattack had been so much part and parcel of the game for so long that the parties involved scarcely took offense, at least not in public. Some of the drafts of memoranda and countermemoranda have survived and it is interesting to see that derogatory statements were usually crossed out before the document was made public. Let us first hear what Buzzi had to say about the project of his most dangerous competitor.[9] His closely written five-page statement is contracted here into a few sentences. Buzzi's first point and one of central importance is that in his view Castelli's project was not uniform with the existing body of the Cathedral (fig. 65). The main reason it had been decided to abandon the Roman project was its lack of uniformity with the rest of the cathedral. Now Castelli committed a similar error by making the columns of the main order too small: their height is only two-thirds of that of the inside piers. They may appear large enough in the drawing, but in reality they would be much too small, especially if one considers that such architectural elements appear even smaller than they are when they are looked at in the open air. Another reason why the Roman project has been abandoned is a technical problem: the quarrying of marble of sufficient length for the cornice. Castelli repeats the old mistake. Other points of criticism are concentrated on the portico, which—according to Buzzi—makes no sense; on the balustrade with the small-scale pyramidal baluster motifs which interfere with the view from the gallery; and on the second order which—he finds—has no proper relation to the interior. Like the Roman design, Castelli's façade is too high and hides the most beautiful and most carefully considered part of the old structure; moreover, Buzzi finds that Castelli's façade is not properly linked with the flanks of the cathedral (fig. 66).

Castelli's answer was more than double the length of Buzzi's criticism. He subdivided Buzzi's arguments into eight main points and each main point into a number of subpoints.[10] His answer to Buzzi's first point began as follows: "There is not a single part or architectural member in my design that does not harmonize and is not uniform with the rest of the building." As usual the guiding principle is uniformity of style, but as you see there were divergent opinions about how to arrive at consistency of style. Castelli goes on to explain that from the uniform base that is carried around the entire structure to the consoles on which the statues are standing and to their little Gothic roofs, there is unison. Point two: The height of the main tier is determined by the position of the window above the main entrance. One can see from the section (fig. 65), which Castelli published in 1651, that the window is in the correct position to supply maximum light to the vault of the nave. Castelli also observes correctly that if he had made the main order higher, the window would also have to be moved up and he is quite right in remarking that in some projects it reaches half above the vault of the nave. Next he explains, again quite correctly, that no old author on architecture maintains that there must be a correspondence of measurements between the inside and the outside. He cites Bramante, Pellegrini, and others, who often placed the smaller order outside. He argues that the decisive point is to achieve harmony between exterior and interior and satisfy the eye of the beholder. In support of his own comparatively small main order he can adduce some façade projects for the cathedral in which the order is even smaller, for example in Tolomeo Rinaldi's project (fig. 41) and even in some projects of the famous Ricchino, as he calls him (fig. 28). The considerable reduction of the height of his own columns as compared with earlier projects was also determined by the fact that the gentlemen of the Fabbrica wanted to see the column shafts made of one piece of marble, which in the past had led to almost insoluble problems. On and on he goes, pedantically rejecting Buzzi's argumentation point by point. But then one comes across an almost humorous touch, for after all his well-aimed polemics he reverses his position and offers to make the principal order as high as the piers of the nave without otherwise changing his design, if this should be the wish of the Chapter.

Castelli continues by brushing off Buzzi's technical question regarding the length of the piece of marble needed for the cornice as a senseless sophism and argues that from the gallery one would look not at near objects but at views in the distance. To Buzzi's criticism of the order of the second tier he also has his answer ready. One of the points he makes is that it is evident, even to people with poor understanding (an offensive phrase that he crossed out), his project corresponds to the rules of art and is well founded. The appeal to the rules of art and to reason, here used in defense of a picturesque Gothic manner, belongs, of course, to the armory of Renaissance theory. Castelli had shown that his main order was in keeping with the rest of the building; now he shows that the second order was in keeping with the first "alla Gotica." Other points Castelli made are of lesser interest to us; at the end he comes back to his principal argument: a disinterested consideration of his project (he maintains) will find that each part corresponds "in ragione"—which means logically or judiciously—with the Gothic fabric; hence there can be no possible reason for any objection to his design.

Let me now turn from Buzzi's criticism to Ricchino's, which is, to a large extent, of a technical nature.[11] Ricchino points out, for instance, that since the columns of the portico would stand some distance away from the wall of the church, new foundations would have to be dug for them; he cannot imagine how Castelli will handle the different heights of vault which would result from the different heights of the Gothic arches; he is afraid that the projection of the portico will interfere with the visibility of the entire height of the orders of the second tier; and so forth. His only aesthetic criticism concerns the shape of the gable which according to him cannot make *un bell'effetto* ("a beautiful impression"). What is remarkable is that Ricchino does not object to a Gothic design as such. One might even say that this fact alone gives one the impression that the advocates of a classical solution were in full retreat. Castelli's answer to Ricchino, once again a document of almost ten closely filled pages, need not detain us;[12] suffice it to mention that the key monuments he adduces for his defense are not other Gothic buildings, but by and large the surviving structures of ancient Rome of which he had a remarkable knowledge.

The result of this first round was a draw. The Deputies realized that procedure had to be changed. It seems they agreed that the classical design was out for good and that the decision lay between the projects of Buzzi and of Castelli. It was for this reason that an engraving of Castelli's design was needed. When it was at hand at the end of 1651 (fig. 67), a memorable inquiry was set on foot. Over the next couple of years a number of specialists were sent engravings of both Buzzi's (fig. 61) and Castelli's projects and their opinion was requested. Among the dozen people eventually asked were the two architects of greatest international reputation at that moment, namely Baldassare Longhena, the architect of S. Maria della Salute in Venice, and the great Giovan Lorenzo Bernini; they as well as a few minor figures sent their responses in the course of 1652. The next group of specialists, who answered two years later, is scarcely known today, and need not be mentioned. The odds were heavily in favor of Castelli. Longhena, too, preferred Castelli, but requested some changes.

The most important answer was, of course, Bernini's. It is not unknown, but has rarely been mentioned and, for reasons, I will give shortly, has never been fully understood. Bernini's letter of 10 March 1652 begins:[13] "I liked the two designs, one by Signor Castelli, the other by Signor Buzzi for the façade of Milan Cathedral. . . . In such matters one is well advised not to deceive oneself with the charm and beauty of details, but to mind the handling of the whole to which the architect has to direct all his attention. When at the first instant the eye meets a form that satisfies by its contour and fills the beholder with admiration, then the aim of art has been achieved." This flow of general wisdom is not without interest: it seems characteristic of Bernini's, in the true sense impressionist and subjectivist, philosophy of art. He continues: "To explain myself better in the present case, it seems to me that two campanili proportionate to the height and grandeur of this structure should be erected at the sides; they would appropriately accompany the vastness and the great bulk of the rest of the building. . . . And since the façade of Signor Castelli pleases me very much indeed (for it is expressed in an architectural manner that will add new riches and nobility to the existing structure) I would say—if I am permitted to do so—that before finishing a work of such fame and importance, he should make another design adding campanili in which the style of his façade design be continued. The project as a whole would then have the required splendor." There are a few more sentences that contribute points we can omit here. Thus, even Bernini, a purist, not to say classicist, in architectural matters, accepted Castelli's quaint Gothic and even invited him to go one better by adding campanili.

But apart from this illuminating fact, his letter "looked upon as a whole" (to use Bernini's own language) is scarcely adequate. Also, not counting the introductory civility, he never mentions Buzzi's project at all. Now the explanation for the weaknesses of the letter is contained in a note by Cardinal Prince Teodoro Trivulzio, a member of the Milanese Cathedral Chapter. This memo or rather draft of a letter preserved in the archive of the Fabbrica has never been published.[14] Somewhat contracted, it reads as follows: "As I have written, I took the two designs of the façade to the Signor Cavalier Bernini. . . . He said to me that one of the two designs, namely that without campanili, was by Francesco Castelli. The other, by Carlo Buzzi, had campanili according to his information. But the design he was given showed the side elevation and not the façade of the Cathedral (fig. 63). If he is expected to comment on Buzzi's project the correct design must be sent to him. Moreover, he wants to know exactly what the Deputies desire: do they want him simply to state whether these projects contain or do not contain shortcomings or should he also state his preference and declare which of the two was more beautiful. In sum, he is requesting full guidance."

The deputies did not feel that they should act hastily upon Cardinal Trivulzio's information. The next we hear in this matter was almost exactly four years later when (on 9 April 1656) Bernini addressed a letter to Cardinal Trivulzio[15] in which he acknowledged the receipt of what he called the "Book of the Designs for the Façade of Milan Cathedral that contains all proposals, opinions, memoranda, and engravings in this matter." This can only be the collection of pamphlets which were issued together under the title *Per la facciata del Duomo*, but without date. This collection, known only in a very few copies (one in the British Museum was destroyed in the last war) seems to have impressed Bernini enormously. In any case, his letter to the cardinal is most carefully styled and he appended to it a closely argued memorandum. The most notable passage of the letter says that since the Roman project by Pellegrini has been definitely rejected, the decision lies between Castelli's and Buzzi's projects. "I find," he wrote, "that Castelli's project is being approved and praised by some of the first architects of our time (as their memoranda in the book you sent me attest, an opinion to which I too subscribe). But doubts fall upon Buzzi's project, which, in contrast to everyone's expectation, without general approval and a definitive design, one continues to build day by day like a vulgar structure, and hence I will comment only on his project in the appended memorandum." The project Bernini is talking about, and on which he is commenting, was Buzzi's last, that of 1653, which, as we saw at the end of the last chapter, served as a basis for the slowly advancing execution (fig. 60).

Bernini's memorandum is really a remarkable document, too long —about fifteen hundred words—to do more than give the gist of it here. It is generally acknowledged—Bernini says—that the substance of architecture consists in order, symmetry, disposition, distribution, eurythmy, decorum, and light. These are all terms deriving from Vitruvius and firmly anchored in the classical theory of architecture. For Bernini as for most of his contemporaries the touchstone of good architecture lay in the satisfactory application of the principles encompassed by these terms. Thus one has to test to what extent Buzzi's design fulfilled their challenge; and so he runs through one term after another. The first one, *ordine*—order: there is none in this façade. For Bernini order consists in what we would now call a modular architecture (fig. 62). But Buzzi's continuous piers without breaks do not supply a basic measure, valid throughout the entire façade. The incompatibility of the narrowness of the piers with their extravagant height is alone a sign of basic disorder. He discusses the principle of order in great detail and concludes that the design consists of an aggregate of incompatible elements.

Bernini proceeds to the second essential, symmetry, which means for him that all members have a proportionate relationship of length, width, and height. In Bernini's view, Buzzi's project consists entirely of disproportionate members. Thus the doors are disproportionately small in relation to the height of the piers, whereas the windows that are planned (he means, of course, the Gothic windows of Buzzi's third design) are too long and have no relationship to the windows and doors underneath. In fact, Gothic windows over Roman ones are quite impossible. "Poor architecture—he is killing it!" Bernini exclaims.

Dispositione—disposition—concerns the arrangements of members in a building in such a way that everything appears *direttamente formato* (which might perhaps be translated: that everything appears to be the result of a natural process). Buzzi's façade has no raison d'être as a façade; it cannot even be said that it incorporates an original idea, for it is simply an imitation of the sides of the building. This is, according to Bernini, unseemly, for a façade must be of a manner and invention quite different from the rest of the structure. Buzzi's aggregate of accidents cannot really be called a façade.

Eurythmy and decorum, too, (which, Bernini maintains, are almost synonyms in art terminology) one seeks in vain in this façade. Eurythmy and decorum are nothing but a concert or harmony of all the parts so that they form an indivisible and elegant whole to which one cannot add and from which one cannot remove anything. Like Leon Battista Alberti long before him, Bernini calls this harmony the one and all of art. But how can one talk of eurythmy in front of Buzzi's junction of two different kinds of architecture, the Roman and the Gothic. In a case such as this the parts must be discrete and not continuous. He goes on: "The Gothic parts should, as far as possible, reveal a typological bond with the Roman ones, so that there is no clash of styles. Buzzi's project is more Gothic than Castelli's and hence the dissonances between the two styles are more obvious in Buzzi's case. His design misses that well-adjusted and concordant blend of both manners which one discovers in Castelli's project. Castelli has demonstrated with ingenuity and singular understanding how to join the two styles proportionally and harmoniously and in his case the existing Roman parts are enclosed by Gothic work that is sufficiently isolated and distinct, so that the eye scarcely becomes aware of the stylistic mixture." Bernini then expresses his distress about the progressive destruction of the elegant pilasters (built by Ricchino) and their replacement by Buzzi's long wallstrips.

There is finally a brief note concerning Bernini's last term: light. His dislike of the Buzzi project goes so far that he even criticizes the large west window (that Buzzi had incorporated in his third design) because, he says, it will transmit the rays of the sun to the farthest part of the church and will be so blinding as to make it impossible to see anything.

It seems to me that we can now understand why Castelli's project was such a success: in contrast to Buzzi's, it was measurable by criteria belonging to classical theory. Castelli's design consisted of discrete units (such as two distinct tiers) and also of distinct parts (such as recognizable orders and horizontal breaks) and was therefore more easily digestible for the seventeenth-century beholder. In historical perspective Buzzi, who challenged all classical concepts and conventions, represents a progressive point of view in contrast to Castelli, Bernini, and the advocates of Castelli's project who defended a more conservative position.

We have no document that would tell us how the Deputies reacted to Bernini's memorandum, but we may hazard a guess. They probably did not expect such absolute support for Castelli's project and such uncompromising hostility toward Buzzi's. There is no doubt that they regarded Bernini as supreme judge: for this reason they had sent him the entire bulky documentation and for this reason they wanted him to stop in Milan on his return from Paris in 1665,[16] but this clever idea miscarried. In any case, they must have been very shaken by his verdict. You may recall that the execution of Buzzi's Gothic pilaster strips was suddenly interrupted and, in fact, never touched again until 1807. There can have been only one reason for the sudden cessation of work, namely the bombshell of Bernini's memorandum. This spells the end of a most important episode in the history of the cathedral façade. Or perhaps not quite, for the further history of projects cannot be dissociated from Buzzi and Castelli.

The first result was three projects by an anonymous Jesuit; one of them bears the following inscription: "This project is arranged in such a way that the part begun according to Buzzi's design can be maintained as will be noticed at the sides of the main portal. But the elevation as a whole is very different which will easily be demonstrated by a confrontation of both projects" (fig. 69). These projects offer an amusing compromise; they demonstrate that what one had learned from Castelli's project could be applied to Buzzi's pilaster strips abandoned in the middle of construction. One can adapt these fragments to the size of classical orders with capitals, one can introduce horizontal breaks, Baroque scrolls, and even campanili, and yet convey a distinct awareness of the Gothic sweep of Buzzi's pilaster strips: in this way uniformity of style with the main structure can be fully obtained. One can even, as a second project shows (fig. 70), vary the proportions of the orders considerably over the same plan. Or if desired, one can return to the Pellegrini-Ricchino solution of placing freestanding columns in front of the pilasters and achieve a Gothic result by means of a classical order with fluted columns (fig. 71). The interest in this architect's ideas is, of course, a purely academic one. His projects look like the outpourings of a cabinetmaker's imagination and had no chance of being taken seriously.

As already mentioned, after 1656 there occurred a very long interval in the affairs of the façade. It lasted until 1733 and was interrupted only by the halfhearted attempt to get Bernini to Milan in 1665 and by the abortive attempt to obtain a design in 1688 from Carlo Fontana in Rome. Fontana was then at the height of his career and was widely regarded as the greatest Italian architect alive.

In December 1732 the Deputies decided to finish the façade in preference to any other work at the cathedral.[17] Now in the 1720s and early 1730s Fontana's mantle had been transferred to his pupil Filippo Juvarra, a Piedmontese court architect at Turin, and Juvarra was asked for a design. He complied and in the summer of 1733 the deputies had before them a design by him with alternative solutions, namely with and without portico.[18] Unable to come to a decision, they all went to study the problem on the spot, but even then no unanimity of opinion was reached. Whereupon it was resolved to invite Juvarra to come to Milan and help reach a decision together with four carefully selected Milanese architects: Carlo Giuseppe Merlo, Marco Bianco, Francesco Croce, and Antonio Quadrio. A meeting was summoned for 21 August, but neither Juvarra nor Merlo could attend. During the meeting three proposals were submitted: to build the façade in the Roman style with composite order, in the Gothic style, or in a mixed style. Again, no majority opinion could be achieved and it was decided to canvass the views of the Archbishop, the judicature, and the public. In short, one was back at a position that, it seemed, had long been resolved, for both Buzzi's and Castelli's projects were in a mixed style. A month later (on 17 September) the Marchese Pallavicini, who conducted the correspondence with Juvarra, received a letter from him in which he declared his readiness to make a design for the façade in the Gothic style (although this was contrary to his previously expressed opinion).

Unfortunately, Juvarra's contributions to the façade have not yet been traced and it is questionable whether his designs are still in existence, but the problem of the façade was on the books once more and some of the members of the Juvarra committee felt encouraged to try their hand at a project. One of these, by Merlo, is known and is probably datable 1734 (fig. 68). Merlo was a busy Baroque architect and one would scarcely have expected his wholehearted attachment to a Gothic solution. In fact, his project shows an alternative design; the left half is in a mixed style, i.e., he suggests setting the existing Roman doors and windows in a Gothic structure; the right half, by contrast, is in a uniform Gothic style with Gothic doors and windows replacing the Roman ones. We can now read such a project like an open book, for it was firmly based on seventeenth-century precedent. Merlo started from Buzzi's last design (fig. 60), to which he owed the simple gable-like diagonal silhouette of the upper part and the large central Gothic window, here somewhat set back so as to form a niche and allow room for an equestrian statue on a large base. (The figure has been recognized as that of St. Ambrose, Bishop of Milan and Doctor of the Church, fighting his enemies at the battle of Parabiago.) For the rest, Merlo was much indebted to Castelli, above all for the portico, which is here fully developed in depth rather than being shallow as Castelli's (fig. 67), and also for the gallery and thus for the horizontal barrier. By representing in his drawing the transept and the *Tiburio* as well, Merlo demonstrated the complete uniformity of his façade with the old structure together with the triumphant assertion of the *Tiburio*. Merlo's façade would be low enough not to interfere with the visibility of the *Tiburio*, which was always regarded as the principal feature of the exterior. But a one-dimensional design does not, of course, represent the view the beholder would enjoy from the piazza in front of the cathedral.

At this point I want to interpolate an anonymous design, the style of which suggests a date in the 1730s; it may well be by another member of the Juvarra committee, namely Marco Bianco (fig. 72). At this historic moment it was quite unique, although Bianco (if he is the author) may have employed motifs from one of the missing Juvarra designs. In any case, at present it seems to be the only project of this period in *stile romano*. Bianco was born in Rome and may well have studied with Carlo Fontana. The use that the architect made of freestanding columns, especially in the central bay, points to a strong Fontana influence. But whether or not this design is by Bianco (who has some respectable buildings in Milan to his credit that support the attribution) the project reveals an independent mind who had the courage to start right at the beginning and to recommend a completely uniform façade of uncompromising modernity.

Another project in a fanciful Gothic or rather mixed manner, a strange freak, caused some stir (fig. 77). The author of the project was a young enthusiast, Antonio Maria Vertemate Cotognola, who was born near Milan in 1704 and died in Rome in 1737. We first hear about this project in February 1735 when a document tells us that he had spontaneously made a design, but that, unless it was chosen for execution, he did not expect to receive any remuneration.[19] Nonetheless, after his sudden death the Chapter decided to pay his widow a fair amount of money—an indication that the design was taken seriously. Other drawings by Vertemate Cotognola show that he intended to preserve the Roman doors and windows. Again he was indebted to Castelli for the idea of the portico (fig. 67) and to Buzzi for the motif of the tower, the large central window, and the pilaster strips on high bases (fig. 62), but the horizontal caesuras such as the capitallike features and the balcony could scarcely have been done without Castelli's example. Vertemate enriched his design with a wealth of unashamedly Baroque motifs, especially statuary. In addition, he planned, anachronistically, an octagonal Baroque dome with Gothic detail over the center bay of the portico, and provided some Gothic features which in isolation one could easily mistake for Victorian. Before discussing a more serious attempt to resolve the impasse, it should be mentioned that after the failure to attract Juvarra to Milan (he had gone to Madrid in 1735 where he died the following year) an attempt was made to secure the services of Nicola Salvi. In 1732 Salvi had won the competition for the erection of the Fontana Trevi in Rome and this established his international reputation. So, in 1738 he was invited to come to Milan for two years, primarily in order to correct Vertemate Cotognola's design. Negotiations dragged on until 1744 when Salvi finally declined because of failing health.[20]

The Deputies immediately started negotiating with Luigi Vanvitelli, who was just beginning to gain general recognition. He came to Milan in 1745, stayed there for a few months, made an impressive design, and became the focus of a fascinating controversy (fig. 73).

The pedigree of Vanvitelli's design is obvious: preservation of Roman doors and windows, portico, an order of corkscrew columns which carry pointed arches and a dwarf order, the long gallery across the façade and twin pinnacles at each end—all this stems from Castelli (fig. 67). But the second tier is very different; it is raised above a high base, has a very high Gothic central niche with a stepped pedestal leading into it, upon which is placed a statue of the Virgin, to whom the Cathedral is dedicated. Ever since Buzzi's third project (fig. 60) and Merlo's niche with the equestrian statue in this position (fig. 68), the motif was in the air. But the side bays with Gothic tracery functioning as transparent screens, the horizontals above, interrupted by the triangular gable—all this was new and interesting and the repeated, strongly speaking horizontals give the design a very special stamp, quite different from all the Gothic or mixed projects we have seen.[21] The high quality of this design is best revealed by Vanvitelli's preparatory sketch, which Karl Noehles discovered in the Albertina in Vienna (fig. 74). Here, in the view from the side, the unity of the concept is most striking. One is immediately reminded of scenographic studies, but among Juvarra's theater designs such Gothic fantasies are not at all rare. We can also see in this sketch that Vanvitelli's façade would have been much higher than the Gothic structure behind.

Merlo and Francesco Croce were invited to comment in writing on Vanvitelli's design. Both were Milanese architects of high standing, and both had submitted designs themselves. Instead of writing a memorandum, Merlo demonstrated in a sheet of drawings that Vanvitelli's corkscrew columns were disagreeing with the Gothic structure both in form and size and showed in a side view of the cathedral that Vanvitelli's portico was too low while the façade as a whole was too high (fig. 75). He juxtaposed a side view of his own design (fig. 76) and this made obvious that he had these matters much on his mind: the portico blends in with the older parts, and the overall height is just right and does not appear to obstruct the view of the tower.

Croce responded to the invitation by writing a long memorandum. On 20 September 1745 he submitted thirty-four objections to Vanvitelli's project to the Fabbrica.[22] Vanvitelli was very busy and could not answer immediately. But the criticism must have rankled, and as a point of honor he could not remain silent. His reply arrived in Milan on 20 February 1751, five and a half years after the attack.[23] It had the length of a small volume and was a masterpiece in the art of controversy. It is not necessary to enlarge on this controversy in any detail, because basically the character and range of arguments had scarcely changed in all those years. Croce had invoked constantly the authority of Vitruvius against Vanvitelli's disposition of columns, his intercolumniations, the relation of the freestanding columns to those attached to the wall, and so forth. But his main point consisted in accusing Vanvitelli of having designed a façade in a Gothic style that was out of tune with the rest of the structure and, in addition, that his façade was much too high and thus was hiding the most beautiful parts of the old church.

Three more names have to be mentioned before we come to the end of this story. The year 1746 saw a design by Giovanni Battista Riccardi, a minor figure in Milanese architectural history (fig. 82). His design is eminently sensible and, obviously, he had made a close study of previous projects. He planned a portico. For the Gothic front he used Buzzi's high pedestals and even the overlong pilaster strips without capitals (fig. 62). The transparent tracery along the diagonal sides of the gables stem from Buzzi and Merlo (fig. 68), and he also incorporated Buzzi's Gothic windows in the side bays of the upper tier. There are horizontal breaks at the height of the balcony, and the crowning part of the design is also horizontal and broken only by the triangular gable. Evidently, the rectangular second tier is in many ways indebted to Vanvitelli's project.

Much more interesting are two designs by one of the greatest architects of the later eighteenth century, the Turinese Bernardo Vittone (fig. 79). His two designs are also datable in 1746, but we know them only from the engravings Vittone himself published in his architectural treatise of 1766 (figs. 78, 80). Both designs have tall companili, the one with the winding gangway along the upper part being to a certain extent indebted to Buzzi. But in other respects the designs are scarcely reminiscent of previous projects. Vittone was, it seems, interested in recreating an immensely rich High Gothic façade architecture, of French rather than Italian pedigree. In both cases he tried to string together towers and façade by strong vertical motifs, but in other respects the two designs differ considerably. In a sense the design with the large unifying triangular gable is more sober than the other one with the richly broken silhouette and an unbelievable amount of decorative detail. Some may shake their heads in front of such designs, yet they represent a distinct and important stage in the Gothic revival when style was regarded as a lively and changeable convention in constant flux. Thus Vittone, who was a keen and precise observer, did not mind adding to the Gothic repertory new forms, some of which have an almost Art Nouveau flavor about them.

Finally, turning from Vittone in 1746 to Giulio Galliori in 1786–87, one is amazed by the change from a picturesque baroque or rococo Gothic to a temperate, dry neoclassical Gothic—so reasonable that it makes one almost yawn (fig. 81). As we have said, Galliori was Cathedral Architect during a critical period, from 1773 to 1795. It is interesting to observe the reasonable union of so many motifs we know very well: the preservation of the Pellegrini-Ricchino doors and windows (fig. 44); the columns with capitals corresponding to those in the interior; the decisive horizontal barrier (stemming from Castelli: fig. 67); the large Gothic window of the second tier and the ascending diagonal silhouettes, both deriving from Buzzi (fig. 62); and finally the high central portion which would not have been possible without Vanvitelli's (fig. 73) and Riccardi's projects (fig. 82). The only new element here is the reduction of the portico—usually running along the whole length of the façade—to the central bay. This had the aesthetic advantage of emphasizing the central area, spatially as well as by the feature of the twin columns, not to mention the considerable lowering of expense.

After Galliori's project, there follow in quick succession those by Leopoldo Pollak (fig. 84), Luigi Cagnola (fig. 83), and Felice Soave (fig. 85), which return more and more to Buzzi's third project. As early as 1797 General Bonaparte (then master of Lombardy) had shown an interest in the completion of the façade.[24] As emperor, he gave orders in 1805[25] to get on with the job. Not that the Milanese buried their time-honored dissensions, but they had to comply. Under Carlo Amati, cathedral architect from 1806 to 1813, the façade was finished. With slight changes, it corresponds to Buzzi's last project (figs. 5 and 60). Thus the (in a sense) most reasonable seventeenth-century project prevailed.

But the completion of the façade was not the end of the story. Right from the beginning the lack of a campanile was strongly felt. Moreover, the Victorian age could not stomach the mixture of Roman and Gothic styles. Hence the fantastic idea to pull down the present façade and replace it by a worthy Gothic one. In 1883 an open competition for a suitable design was arranged. As far as numbers go it was an enormous success: 120 elaborate projects reached Milan. Architects from France, England, Germany, and Russia competed with Italians (figs. 86, 87). It was only then made manifest that most planners had lost touch with reality and surrendered themselves to romantic dreams. However, the sole meager result of these incredible efforts was an increase in decorative features. In 1927 the simple pyramidal crowning motifs were replaced by more ornate tracery work (fig. 8). But even this was not the end. In 1938 Mussolini approved the construction of a Gothic campanile next to the cathedral; it was to be finished in 1942 (fig. 88). Only the war prevented this piece of fascist megalomania from going up; the campanile was to be 540 feet high, the highest in the world.

Compared with such absurd modern ideas the seventeenth-century architects were clearly guided by a much better understanding of the obligations which the existing Gothic body of the cathedral imposed upon their designs for the façade. Surely, their terms of reference brought them much closer to the situation with which they had to deal than one would have expected.

CHAPTER **IV**

S. Petronio
at Bologna and
Florence Cathedral

OUR STUDY of the projects for the façade of Milan Cathedral
have revealed two distinct Gothic trends toward the middle of
the seventeenth century: one that might be termed "orthodox" found
expression in Carlo Buzzi's design (fig. 61); the other that was non-
conventional could be traced in Francesco Castelli's design (fig. 64).
One might differentiate between a traditionally and archaeologically
inclined style and a free and picturesque one or, as some contemporaries had it, an ancient Gothic versus a new Gothic manner.
Contemporary reactions, moreover, revealed that it was easier for
seventeenth-century critics to understand and appreciate Castelli's
baroque-Gothic than Buzzi's neo-Gothic—for the simple reason that
one had critical terms of reference for Castelli's but not for Buzzi's
Gothic. Bernini's memorandum revealed that Castelli's Gothic was
acceptable because it accorded with classical standards and concepts
which had retained unchallenged validity in Italy for the three hundred years from 1450 to 1750. Nevertheless, Buzzi's design or designs
as well as Buzzi's own defense of them showed that, guided by the
idea of concordance or stylistic uniformity, a positive approach to the
Gothic style was feasible. Buzzi's intense study of the old cathedral, a
preliminary to his neo-Gothic design, brought about an awareness of

the beauty enshrined in the old German manner—a beauty to which the classical terms of reference were scarcely applicable.

At this point I would like to recall that during the Gothic period of the cathedral prolonged discussions had taken place about the geometrical principles which were to inform the structure; that Cesariano handed a knowledge of these principles on to later generations, and that it was always realized that even the Gothic style—at Milan in any case—was dependent on strictly applied geometrical laws (figs. 24, 25). It was this idea that helped to make Milanese Gothic palatable to the seventeenth century.

But Milan Cathedral was not an entirely isolated case. There was at least one other great church, namely S. Petronio at Bologna, where we encounter closely related problems (figs. 89, 93). S. Petronio has attracted more international attention than Milan Cathedral and it is for this reason and not for lack of intrinsic interest that it will be discussed less thoroughly than Milan. After the contributions by Springer, Weber, Panofsky, Zucchini, and Bernheimer, comparatively little remains to be done.[1] Finally, in 1960 Paul Frankl dedicated to this question a few splendid pages in the book to which I referred in chapter one.

There must have been a give and take between Milan and Bologna over a long period of time, and, indeed, from the very beginning the connection is well documented. The first architect of S. Petronio was a certain Antonio di Vincenzo. He was sent to Milan in 1390 to find out what the Milanese were doing and one of his sheets with sketches after the cathedral designs survives in Bologna and, ever since it has become known, has been guarded as a unique treasure (fig. 13). All the other early visual documentation for S. Petronio, the drawings and models, have been irrevocably lost; only the great model of the church, executed much later, in 1514, survives (fig. 90). The Bolognese intended to compete with Florence Cathedral: the project of the church that the burghers of Bologna wanted to build for their patron saint was megalomaniac. The Gothic church would have been over 700 feet long, the length of the transept was to be almost 400 feet and the height of the dome over the crossing was to be 500 feet and would have surpassed that of Florence by one-third. Of all this, just about half the length, namely the nave down to the crossing (370 feet), was executed—and in 1647 the nave was closed by an apse, which buried all dreams of gigantic dimensions; but even the fragment that the visitor to the church sees nowadays is immensely impressive. The present nave is 50 feet wide and 120 feet high (figs. 91, 92). The façade, well known to many of us, was never finished. Its marble incrustation was begun in 1394. The main glory of this unfinished front is, of course, the central portal with Jacopo della Quercia's reliefs along the jambs, and figures in the tympanum executed from 1425 onward. The sculptures of the side portals date a hundred years later.

Before discussing the projects for the façade, preserved in fairly large numbers and mainly belonging to the sixteenth century, we will concentrate on another problem, namely the finishing of the nave. In about 1440 the nave was given a provisional flat ceiling. There was a consensus of opinion that for reasons of uniformity of style a Gothic quadripartite ribbed vault would eventually have to be provided. This work was begun by Francesco Morandi, called Terribilia, who was Cathedral Architect from 1568 to his death in 1603: he started vaulting at the apse end in 1587.

At this stage an extraordinary and wholly unexpected thing happened. A man of the people named Carlo Carazzi, called Cremona, a tailor by profession, challenged what the Cathedral Architect had been doing and accused him of having disregarded the requirements of medieval triangulation. Cremona pointed out that Terribilia's nave was too low; its correct height ought to have been determined by the equilateral triangle, one side of which has to equal the entire width of the church. S. Petronio, he declared, had been based not on the proportions of the Roman style, but on those of an entirely different class of architecture commonly called German manner. The principles of this manner can be derived from Cesariano (he had of course Cesariano's analysis of the proportional system of Milan Cathedral in mind).

Cremona had read and digested the great manuals on architectural theory and so he propounded that beauty consisted in the correct relationship of all the elements of a building to each other. This implied, in his view, that a building must be continued according to the system that had informed it at the start. Since S. Petronio was begun in the *maniera tedesca*, i.e., according to triangulation, it must be finished in the same German manner.

At first Terribilia did not take his antagonist too seriously. He called his the frivolous voice of someone who had no idea what architecture was about. Nevertheless, he was angry and steamrollered his opponent, not always quite fairly, in a lengthy memorandum. Cremona had adduced Vitruvius and, above all, Alberti as a proof that architecture had to be as rationally and as mathematically organized as music—to which Terribilia answered that those authors did not mean that architecture was a synonym for geometry, music, and philosophy. Among many other points, Terribilia denied that Gothic architects were really excessively fond of triangulation and declared that they dealt with this question rather haphazardly. S. Petronio, moreover, might be called "più tosto architettura abusata che regolata," i.e., misused rather than well controlled architecture.

Well, Cremona did not wait long with *his* response to Terribilia's answer; it was precise and incisive. Meanwhile it became evident that Cremona's arguments had made a great impression. On 17 June 1589 the Bolognese Building Committee received a letter from Cardinal Montalto in Rome saying that he had heard from a variety of sources that the people of Bologna were dissatisfied with the vault of S. Petronio.[2] "I have now confirmation [Montalto continued] that the tailor Carlo Cremona has not only convinced the craftsmen with his triangulation idea, but also many of the first citizens of Bologna and they are now lending the full weight of their authority to Cremona's point of view. Therefore, as President to this structure and as the Holy Father's Deputy in this affair, I declare it necessary to carry out a careful examination of all the facts, in order both to remove dissensions and to give satisfaction to everyone. Further consultations should be transferred to Rome, for Rome, which sets the standards for the whole world, harbors people who should be able to resolve the present controversy." He therefore suggested that Terribilia and Cremona come to Rome at the earliest possible moment, equipped with all the measurements, memoranda, and recommendations, and that first-rate experts examine the problem in the presence of both men.

All this seems to me to be of exceptional interest. Let us see this matter in proper perspective: Not only were the citizens of a large town at loggerheads over the question whether the vault of their great church should be 130 feet high (as their architect had built it) or 33 feet higher (as a layman had made out it should be), but the Vatican regarded the dispute of sufficient importance to want to arbitrate. This is remarkable enough. Moreover, what divided those people was a matter of principle. They did not all file into the church and say: "Terribilia's bay looks too low; it surely ought to be higher"—they were, or professed to be, guided by an abstract idea of how to achieve concordance of all the parts. It is also quite mistaken to regard (as some scholars have done) the advocacy of Gothic orthodoxy as a class problem: that the lower orders rather than the upper strata of society—the wealthy and educated—favored Gothic traditions. We have just seen a clear statement that owing to the support of the tailor's case by many of the first citizens of Bologna the matter had assumed supra-Bolognese implications.

Meanwhile, instead of summoning Terribilia and Cremona to Rome, Cardinal Montalto decreed that one of the two foremost Roman architects, either Domenico Fontana or Giacomo della Porta, ought to go to Bologna so as to come to a decision on the spot. But these two architects were so busy in Rome that they could not leave the city and so the pope himself ordered Martino Longhi, a man of considerable standing in the profession who had just finished the church of S. Girolamo degli Schiavoni in Rome (he died two years later, in 1591), to gather all necessary information in minutest detail in Bologna and return to Rome to report, which he did. Two drafts of a report—similar to each other and unsigned, but in my opinion attributable to Longhi—have survived. He gives his full support to Terribilia's handling of the vault, regards it as suitable and well adjusted to the statical problems of the buildings, and thinks that a heightening of the nave might even endanger the safety of the structure. Although he emphasizes that the points made by the other party are well taken, he also stresses that such mathematical and musical refinements are not always observed, as is made manifest by a great number of noble and praiseworthy buildings. Practice is different from theory and while one may want to dabble in mathematical speculations, practice is the real end of architecture.

Obviously, Longhi was not a man of ideas, and his purely pragmatic approach to architecture was ill suited to pacify Bolognese emotions. Even among Bolognese architects the rift seemed to be unbridgeable. So in 1591 the Bolognese Senate commissioned one of Cremona's partisans, the architect Floriano Ambrosini, to construct two large wooden models (each over four feet high) which would make it possible to see Terribilia's and Cremona's solutions side by side and study them, as it were, in reality. These models survive and are now in the museum of S. Petronio (figs. 94, 95). Each model shows one bay of the nave and aisles in a transverse section and it is very easy to perceive the difference in the height of the respective naves. They are related almost precisely as four to five; expressed in meters, Terribilia's nave is forty meters high and Cremona's would have been just over fifty meters high.

In order to clarify further and, in addition, perpetuate, what the models demonstrated, Ambrosini had them represented together in a well-known engraving, dated 1592 (fig. 96). He dedicated the engraving to the governing body of the city and demonstrated most instructively the disputed matter. In the foreground we see Cremona's bay, the height of which is determined by the equilateral triangle; and equilateral triangles, half the size of the major one, determine the height of the aisles. Behind Cremona's high bay appears Terribilia's much lower one which, as you see, is not determined by a regular geometrical figure. The perpendicular from the base of the equilateral triangle to its apex shows the inscribed measurement 133½ piedi, i.e., Bolognese feet, while the perpendicular from the floor to the vault of Terribilia's bay has the inscribed figures: 105½ "feet."

Even with this critical material—the models and the didactic engraving—at hand, the two contending parties could not see eye to eye. In the end Pope Clement VIII himself had to cut this Gordian knot by prohibiting the continuation of work at the vault of the nave. This was in 1594, and over half a century went by before the affair got moving once again; it was only in 1648 that the vaulting of the nave was resumed. But important steps had been taken in 1625. At that moment Girolamo Rainaldi was asked for an expert opinion. Girolamo, the father of the much greater Carlo Rainaldi, enjoyed a considerable reputation in his day. He was born in Rome in 1570, had studied architecture with Domenico Fontana (the architect of Pope Sixtus V), had been appointed Architect to the City of Rome in 1602, and had large commissions in and near Rome; in addition, he was also much in demand in the north of Italy: he had commissions at Parma, Piacenza, Modena, and, above all, at Bologna. In this town he had recently designed the church of S. Lucia, the façade of which was begun in 1623, but remained a fragment. Thus the Bolognese knew and apparently liked him, and they must have thought that a man so much in demand in the big world must be an outstanding architect. They also asked him in 1626 for a design for the façade of S. Petronio, which I shall discuss later (fig. 111). As regards the vault he seemed to have had a comparatively free hand, for scarcely any of the champions of the old dispute of 1589–92 could have been alive anymore; one would also expect that after the death of Terribilia and Cremona the whole issue would have lost something of its urgency. Rainaldi laid down his opinion in a memorandum of May 1625 in which he praised Terribilia's handling of the vault;[3] yet he must have been aware that an overwhelming feeling for the validity of Cremona's cause was still animating the public. So he suggested that the height of Terribilia's vault be increased by 8½ Bolognese feet (or over 3 meters) to 114 feet. The Bolognese were not satisfied and step by step Rainaldi agreed to go higher—to 120 feet. This height was almost exactly halfway between the Terribilia vault of 105½ and the Cremona vault of 133½ feet. This compromise was acceptable and in 1648 a Francesco Martini, at that time Architect to S. Petronio, began vaulting the first bay from the entrance in accordance with Rainaldi's project. Eight years later, having arrived at Terribilia's vault, he had to dismantle it and rebuild it 5 meters higher.

One can give more than a single interpretation to this strange story. It is evident, however, that the Bolognese of the second quarter of the seventeenth century were less punctilious in observing the fine points of the Gothic tradition than many of their forebears at the end of the sixteenth century. But one cannot say that they only paid lip service to that tradition or else they would not have agreed to spending good money on the destruction of a perfectly satisfactory vault. Although, like the earlier generation, they must still have felt that professional expertise was less compelling than the time-honored demand for stylistic uniformity, they were now lacking a personality imbued with Cremona's fanaticism and, moreover, were—as the result shows—not entirely unimpressed by the authority wielded by the Architect of the City of Rome. But not unlike Martino Longhi in his time, the architect of the Roman people was scarcely in touch with the important events in Rome in the second quarter of the seventeenth century; he was eternally dedicated to Mannerist traditions, which he carried over into the seventeenth century, and altogether his style was somewhat outmoded. Again, not unlike Martino Longhi, he was a pragmatist to whom concession and compromise were second nature. Thus, he was scarcely the right man to dispel the ideological fog that had enveloped the question of the Gothic vault. But his compromise solution seems to have satisfied all factions and turned out to be most successful. The interior of S. Petronio is one of the most superb Gothic spaces in Italy (fig. 91). Thus, despite the step-by-step adjustments with which Rainaldi yielded to public pressure (which would seem the death knell to any project) and despite the architect's questionable equipment for his difficult task, no finer Gothic solution could be imagined. This great work of seventeenth-century Gothic is indicative of impressive sensibility under circumstances that all seemed adverse to such a result.

The controversy that we have found in the late sixteenth and the seventeenth century with regard to the vaulting was not at all new at Bologna, where there was a long tradition for intense participation by the public in the affairs of S. Petronio. A memorable situation had arisen at a time when Arduino Arriguzzi held the office of Architect to S. Petronio, from 1507 to 1531. The wooden model of the whole church (fig. 90) was executed during Arriguzzi's tenure of office (1513–16) and it was Arriguzzi who was also responsible for the side portals of the façade; but when the right-hand portal was unveiled in 1520, the public was greatly displeased. In Arriguzzi's own words, "priests, monks, workmen, peasants, weavers, schoolteachers, handymen, and even water carriers" felt entitled to voice criticism and, in fact, succeeded in having the portal torn down and redesigned.[4]

Similar situations also arose in the course of planning the façade of S. Petronio, a matter to which we will now turn. In many ways the problem of the façade designs anticipates the situation at Milan. It was at Bologna that Renaissance architects first struggled with the question of what kind of façade to provide for a great Gothic structure. It was at Bologna that they first investigated the alternatives that offered themselves: to build Gothic for the sake of stylistic conformity; to build classical, i.e., modern, unencumbered by the notion of stylistic unity; or to compromise and suggest a solution that would have enough classical features to make the façade conform to current aesthetic ideals and yet throw in sufficient Gothic motifs to avoid a clash of incompatible styles. These alternatives were clearly seen and discussed in the sixteenth century. There were other characteristic parallels with Milan: above all, it was found that also for S. Petronio the best expert advice was needed and so the greatest living architects were approached and made designs, side by side with local practitioners of much inferior status.

Of the great number of projects for the façade which have survived and are now housed in the Museo di S. Petronio we shall consider only those which are crucial to the period under discussion. In assessing the façade projects, it has always to be kept in mind that Quercia's central portal existed and that, from the 1520s onward, also the side portals had to be taken into account. Another point has to be added. In 1518 the sculptor Domenico da Varignana made a façade design that opened the long series of sixteenth-century projects (fig. 97). It is immediately recognizable that this design (for which art historians could never muster much enthusiasm) represents an attempt to show Gothic features such as the large central window, the ogee arches, and tall buttresses with tabernacle niches placed upon them—in a more or less contemporary setting. Modernity was attempted by studding the façade with rectangular ornamental blocks and by using many horizontal breaks across the buttresses. Strangely enough, this somewhat amateurish design had important consequences, for the *fabbricieri* (or *fabbriceri*, as they were called at Bologna), i.e., the men of the building committee, returned to Varignana's design in the late 1540s, and at that time two rows of blocks with the canopies for statues between them were executed. All later projects had to reckon with this intractable marble decoration, which still survives and which made it virtually impossible to finish the façade. Incidentally, the strange marble decoration has parallels only in Bologna (see Palazzo Fantuzzi-Cloetta, begun in 1517, presumably by Formigine). But Bernheimer may have made a good point when he described these bases as a plastic paraphrase of medieval colored incrustation in Tuscany probably directly derived from Florence Cathedral (fig. 114).[5]

After Varignano's problematical design, one turned to the man who at that moment enjoyed unequalled reputation as an architect, namely Baldassare Peruzzi. In 1521–22 he came to Bologna with three projects, all versions of a mixed solution. The one reproduced here combines two alternatives based on the wedding of Gothic windows, pinnacles, and crockets with a classical triple order which gave the façade a firm three-tier structure (fig. 98); even the strange Gothic tower of the left-hand project combines Gothic windows with a closely-set classical system of orders.

Peruzzi's projects were handed for expert examination to Ercole Seccadenari, a local architect who, at that moment, seemed to be the coming man and who, some years later, in 1530, was indeed appointed Architect to S. Petronio. Now a grotesque situation arose: This greenhorn in architectural matters was sitting in judgment over a great master who, among others, was Deputy Architect to St. Peter's in Rome. Seccadenari praised Peruzzi's designs, called him an *homo da bene* ("a fine fellow") but maintained nevertheless that Peruzzi's projects were of no use because of lack of conformity with the style of the church. Thus we are back to the old problem, to which there was no ready answer. The Bolognese, however, hoped to resolve this impasse by appealing to highest authority. The notary of the Fabbrica was asked to address Michelangelo himself in the name of the *fabbricieri*. The letter, dated 2 July 1522, inviting Michelangelo to survey the problem on the spot, survives,[6] but so far as we know Michelangelo did not even answer it. It would have been interesting to know how he viewed the intractable question of conformity.

For more than twenty years no further progress was made. Then, in the 1540s, the problem was activated again. Shortly before his death in 1546 Giulio Romano was paid for a design that he had made in cooperation with Cristoforo Lombardo, who was Seregni's teacher at Milan and himself a distinguished architect of Milan Cathedral (fig. 99). Their combined effort shows once again a mixture of Gothic windows and pinnacles with classical order. Another project by Giulio Romano alone is overcrowded with reliefs (fig. 100); they are organized in fields framed by orders on which Gothic tabernacle-niches are placed. Alternative crowning features— Gothic canopies and classical obelisks—show that such elements were practically interchangeable in a façade of mixed style.

Giulio Romano's projects were not acceptable. In the same years the *fabbricieri* had also won Vignola.[7] In 1543 they had appointed him Architect to S. Petronio next to the local architect Giacomo Ranuzzi. Vignola made two closely similar projects, both immensely sensible and reasonable and each a kind of dry, sober version of Peruzzi's earlier designs (figs. 101, 103). In any case, Vignola's project is a professional attempt to master the difficulties inherent in the prevailing conditions and solve the problem of conformity. Even though his project may not contain staggeringly new ideas, it is infinitely superior to the inept North Italian design by Ranuzzi, if the later inscription is correct in naming him as the author (fig. 104). Ranuzzi, however, was only interested in ousting his dangerous competitor: in a memorandum he accused Vignola of an infinite number of basic blunders and as a result of these attacks (which continued even after Ranuzzi's death) Vignola was finally dismissed.

The next stage takes us to the most critical decade in the affairs of the façade, the 1570s, i.e., to the period after the marble decoration of the brick wall had been finished to the height of the central portal. The *fabbricieri* commissioned two architects to make new designs: Terribilia, the Architect to S. Petronio, who was responsible for the controversial vault, and Domenico Tibaldi, a younger brother of the much greater Pellegrino Tibaldi, or Pellegrino Pellegrini, well known to us from Milan Cathedral. Both designs incorporate—as one would expect —the then-existing Varignana decoration, both continue the theme of the incrustation in the upper regions of the façade, both designs are predominantly Gothic and show so many common features that they cannot be independent of each other (figs. 102, 105). But Tibaldi's design is more decorative and playful than Terribilia's, and this is most clearly revealed in the form of the gables crowning the circular windows and especially in the gable topping the central bay. One is reminded of the large decorative late-Gothic frames of Venetian paintings.

With these two projects before the *fabbricieri*, their chairman, Count Giovanni Pepoli, decided to take a decisive step in order to prevent a continuation of the eternal controversies. He asked his cousin Fabio Pepoli in Venice to take all the façade projects made to this moment to Palladio—whose reputation had no equal—and ask for his opinion.[8] Palladio immediately volunteered the view that none of the projects was satisfactory and that in order to be able to make some progress one would have to dismantle the marble facing down to the old base. Regarding Tibaldi's and Terribilia's designs, he added that Terribilia's (fig. 102) showed fewer defects than Tibaldi's (fig. 105), but that nonetheless a new design would have to be made.

After further discussions Palladio was warmly invited to come to Bologna and judge the situation on the spot. Probably convinced that he was the man whom Bologna needed, he went there in July 1572, but to his dying day in 1580 he, too, was unable to resolve the S. Petronio problem. On the occasion of his visit he came to the conclusion that Terribilia was not entirely incapable. So before leaving he made a sketch for Terribilia to use for a new design which he was to send to him in Venice. This project, that was dispatched to Palladio before 5 September 1572, is preserved (fig. 106). It is remarkably interesting, for it represents nothing less than a revolution in the façade designs for S. Petronio. Although the Varignana marble incrustation of the lower part was maintained (fig. 97), the façade has taken on a distinctly classical aspect owing to the treatment of the upper part with a combination of a small and large order, of round-headed windows above the side portals, and a so-called Venetian window in the center of the uppermost tier. But more important than all this: instead of the five Gothic triangular gables with forty-five-degree angles (a feature repeated in almost all previous façade projects) we find here fragments of classical pediments over the outer bays and a full classical pediment over the central portion. This motif, so well known from Palladio's church façades, gives emphasis to a horizontal unification of the façade; and this anti-Gothic horizontality is strongly felt in the effective double barrier of the unbroken entablature over the second and third tiers. Pellegrino Pellegrini used exactly the same device for his classical project for Milan Cathedral.

The discussion that arose over this design was long and painful. It was only in November 1577 that Pepoli reported to Palladio that

some professional criticism had been voiced although he, Pepoli himself, was standing firmly behind Palladio's design. In January 1578
Palladio sent Pepoli a carefully considered answer in which he made
eleven separate points.[9] In a famous passage, Palladio emphatically
asserts (or rather reasserts) that "architecture consists in well propor-
tioned relationships," and that it is "these harmonic correspondences
that contain majesty and decorum." By contrast, "the *maniera tedesca*
must be called confusion rather than architecture and his [Palladio's]
critics seem to have studied the German rather than the good manner."

Palladio now regarded it necessary to make a project of his own.
He first thought in terms of modernizing the project Terribilia had
executed in accordance with his directives (fig. 107). He did away
with the Varignana incrustation, replacing it by a classical order, without however altering the essential character of the previous design.
This project was apparently followed by another almost identical one
that only differed with regard to the sculptural decoration. Pepoli sent
this design to a certain Camillo Bolognini, then Bolognese ambassador in Rome, who had the reputation of being a good judge of architecture, and he laid the project before Giacomo della Porta, at that
time Architect to St. Peter's and therefore a man who enjoyed immense
reputation. Porta studied the project for two hours, and although he
overflowed with praise of it, he made a few minor objections.[10]

Perhaps as a result of these new difficulties Palladio decided to
break entirely with the past, to do away not only with the Varignana
decoration, but also with the portals (including Quercia's) and to design a modern façade of the type he had established in S. Francesco
della Vigna, in S. Giorgio Maggiore, and the Redentore. His design
contains two alternatives, two versions of the same thought, namely to
give the church a monumental classical order of giant proportions and
combine it with a subsidiary minor order (fig. 108). But even
this design was superseded by one only preserved in a copy (in an
American private collection) the principal motif of which is a powerful
hexastyle open portico (fig. 109). So, briefly, Palladio's designs
illustrate a progressive breaking away from an attempt to reconcile
his ideas with the traditional and medievalizing features that existed
in the façade of S. Petronio and a turn toward a more and more outspoken advocacy of a purely classical solution to the problem.

Thus, we find a position at Bologna paralleling exactly that in
Milan at the same moment in time. Just as Pellegrini's Milan Cathedral project (fig. 36), so Palladio's S. Petronio project spelled a passing proscription of any compromise with the Gothic manner. It seems

to me that Martino Bassi had knowledge of Palladio's portico project for S. Petronio, for Bassi also advocated a radically classical solution for Milan Cathedral in his portico project of 1590, a decade later (fig. 40).

Despite all this, the situation at Bologna changed much more rapidly than that in Milan. Palladio died in August 1580. In November of the same year the discussion turned once again to the old problem whether the façade should be built *all'antica,* i.e., in classical style, or *alla tedesca,* i.e., in the Gothic manner, or in a mixed style, and the governing body, following the advice of a group of architects, pronounced the verdict that it ought to be built Gothic: the principle of conformity had won. It was decided to have a Gothic design produced that would combine elements from Tibaldi's and Terribilia's projects (figs. 102, 105). This decision found support from the greatest living expert on these matters, Pellegrino Pellegrini. He was approached in 1582 and sent a memorandum to Bologna declaring that a classical façade was infinitely preferable to a Gothic one, but added that if the Bolognese could not afford to pull down what was standing, they should finish the façade in the Gothic manner, because the mixing of styles was the worst mistake one could make.[11]

So everything seemed to be set for a rapid move, but nothing happened for over forty years. We have already heard that Girolamo Rainaldi made a façade design in 1626 (fig. 111). He returned to a mixed-style project, maintained the Varignana incrustation, planned a strongly speaking triple motif of elongated mullioned windows, applied rather emphatic classical orders on three levels, and, in addition, such Renaissance and Baroque elements as triangular and segmental pediments, niches, and scrolls. All this is blended with Gothic pinnacles and finials rising next to bizarre pyramidal shapes. Add the visually impressive crocketlike elements studding the silhouette, and it must be admitted that none of the previous projects approached the exuberant quality of this one. Once again, the striking parallel with Milan cannot be overlooked. Rainaldi's project has a seventeenth-century richness and ebullience that invites comparison with the slightly later Milan design by Castelli (fig. 67). The antipurist tendency of both projects is most marked.

Over a hundred years later we approach the last act. In 1748 Carlo Francesco Dotti,[12] perhaps the most distinguished Bolognese architect of the eighteenth century and known to many of us from the Sanctuary of S. Lucia built by him high above the city, submitted a Gothic façade project that was heavily indebted to Terribilia (fig. 110). As Dotti's own text on the sheet says, the project was in fact meant to be a corrected edition of Terribilia's (fig. 102). As so often, the eighteenth century reverted to the late sixteenth, a phenomenon that has been observed, but perhaps not sufficiently investigated. But then, four years after this exercise in the revival of sixteenth-century Gothic, Dotti made a classical façade design for S. Petronio (fig. 112), the pedigree of which leads us to Roman mid-seventeenth-century Baroque façades: not only the organization of walls and orders in different planes, but above all the concentration of clusters of columns toward the center, leave no doubt about the source of Dotti's inspiration. What is remarkable and perhaps not generally realized is that a first-rate mid-eighteenth-century architect was capable of switching styles with a facility usually associated with the nineteenth century.

At the time of Dotti's first project (in 1748), Mauro Tesi, an interesting artist, tried to promote a project of his for S. Petronio (fig. 113). He was mainly a theatrical designer who had a romantic predilection for extravagant stylistic experiments; he once again started from Terribilia's design, but transformed it in a personal way showing a penchant for decorative forms of his own invention. In contrast to Milan Cathedral, however, no solution was found for S. Petronio that would satisfactorily reconcile the existing lower portion of the façade with a different design in the upper area, and it does not seem astonishing that some minor nineteenth-century architects who made façade projects for S. Petronio could only think in terms of versions of Terribilia's late-sixteenth-century project.

Many modern beholders have taken a liking to the huge unfinished, but immensely impressive brick front of S. Petronio. Many will prefer it to the late-nineteenth-century Gothic façade realized at the Cathedral of Florence (fig. 114). The position of Florence was vaguely similar to that at Milan and at Bologna. The new Florentine Cathedral was begun by Arnolfo di Cambio in the last decade of the thirteenth century, just about a hundred years before Milan Cathedral and S. Petronio. At first the building advanced rapidly, and a start was made on the west façade. After an interruption of more than half a century the façade was continued, but never finished. The appearance of this façade is known from various representations, best of all through a drawing that can probably be dated in 1587 (fig. 115). You see that this Gothic façade was only half finished; it consisted of three canopied portals and, in the fields between them, of niches in several tiers richly decorated with statuary. One can hardly doubt that Varignana took his bearings for his S. Petronio façade design of 1518 from the Gothic

façade of Florence Cathedral (fig. 97). In 1587 Grand Duke Ferdinand I decided that the time had come to pull down the antiquated
Gothic façade and replace it by a modern one. Although the barbarous act of destruction was carried out with Florentine efficiency there
were voices of disagreement: a contemporary diarist, for instance, recorded with utter dismay the destruction of what he called the rich
and beautiful old façade and regarded its loss as an eternal disgrace.[13]
The drawing reproduced was probably made by someone who wanted
to preserve a kind of photographic record of the glory that was doomed
to disappear.

Five renowned Florentine architects were commissioned to represent their ideas for a new façade in wooden models. These models
survived in good condition in the Museo dell'Opera del Duomo and
only suffered damage in the recent disastrous Florentine flood. The
competing architects were Buontalenti, Dosio, Cigoli, Giovanni Bologna, and Don Giovanni de'Medici. The attribution of these models to
the names of architects has caused some confusion which has not yet
been entirely cleared up. The most Mannerist and the most classical
of these models are by Buontalenti and Dosio and both are documented as being from 1589. Buontalenti's model (fig. 116), in three tiers
and a high attic over the first, displays a confusing welter of motifs and
relationships; Dosio's, by contrast, is utterly simple (fig. 117): it is
concentrated in two tiers, has a giant order of Corinthian pilasters below, and telling horizontal breaks. This was the most successful project and once again the comparison with Pellegrini's contemporary
project for Milan Cathedral offers itself (fig. 36).

The question whether or not a small model with the inscription
1596 in the frieze is also by Buontalenti (according to some sources he
had made two models) or by the painter Cigoli, who studied architecture under Buontalenti, has not been decided satisfactorily (fig. 118).
In any case, there are Buontalentesque Cigoli drawings for the façade
in the Uffizi and from them to the wooden model is not an easy but
a possible step.

Giovanni Bologna's participation in the competition, testified to
by various seventeenth-century sources, is now generally accepted (fig.
119). His model is akin to Dosio's and shares in the classicizing taste
around 1600, while Don Giovanni de'Medici's model (fig. 120) is
closely related to Giovanni Bologna's. This Medici prince, Grand Duke
Cosimo I's natural son, was a distinguished amateur practitioner who
supervised most of the large Florentine architectural undertakings at
the beginning of the seventeenth century.

(79)

Despite some considerable differences in style between all these models they have that much in common that they do not take the slightest account of the Gothic body of the church. The hasty destruction of Arnolfo di Cambio's medieval façade had been a sort of overture to these anti-Gothic and implicitly antiuniformity models, none of which was destined to be executed. For well over thirty years nothing happened at all. Then from 1630 onward things began to move again, and in 1633 Grand Duke Ferdinand II came back to Dosio's model (fig. 117), had it slightly modernized and proposed its execution to a committee of experts.[14] Seven of them favored execution, two liked the model but regarded it as unsuitable for the cathedral, and five turned against it: the result was a draw. Among the critics were Coccapani, now practically forgotten, and Gherardo Silvani, Florence's greatest seventeenth-century architect. These two were the only ones who considered the lack of unity between the old building and the new façade a serious shortcoming. Thus in Florence, too, the seventeenth century saw a return to the central question of the Gothic problem. The Grand Duke was impressed and ordered an examination by the prestigious Accademia del Disegno. After protracted planning and replanning the academicians produced a counterproject, of which a wooden model was constructed (fig. 121), and concurrently, in 1635, Gherardo Silvani, Ferdinand II's favorite architect, produced a model of his own (fig. 122).

Opinion favored the Academy project, and the Grand Duke therefore ordered its execution.[15] On 22 October 1636 the foundation stone for this façade was laid. Paradoxically, Silvani was appointed executing architect. Since the Academy project had been preferred to his own, it was only to be expected that he would soon discover so many technical and aesthetic faults in the Academy project that the Grand Duke gave the order to discontinue construction.[16] In fact, the Academy project and Silvani's are closely related. Both are three-tier structures and in both one easily discovers a great many similar motifs, as, for example, the niches for figures framed by pilasters (a motif, incidentally, that was taken over from earlier projects). But the Academy project is not only more logical in an academic sense (for instance, the niche and pilaster motifs are carried on through the three tiers and do not peter out in the third, as in Silvani's model), but it is less adventurous than Silvani's; it is drier and that, I suppose, assured its general acceptance.

It is, however, more interesting and important to note that, in the heat of the many discussions, the academicians once again dropped

any reference to the Gothic style and presented a purely classical design—while Silvani made an attempt, albeit a scarcely successful one,
to introduce a Gothic element in his façade model with the octagonal
side towers, which were inspired by Giotto's Campanile, but they are
not really integrated into the façade design. Silvani paid no more than
lip service to the principle of conformity. It would be worth speculat-
ing on why Milan and Bologna had far outpaced Florence in progress-
ing toward a positive historicizing attitude in relation to the Gothic
style.

When, after two and a half centuries, the Florentines returned
to their cathedral façade, it was a foregone conclusion that it had to be
built in harmony with the rest of the church. Ninety-two Gothic projects were under consideration between 1861 and 1868; the one by De
Fabris, chosen for execution, was built between 1875 and 1887 (fig.
123). Obviously this façade spelled the victory of historicism: everything down to the minutest detail is amply supported by Tuscan precedent.

CHAPTER V

Theory and Practice: Borromini and Guarini; Their Forerunners and Successors

I HAVE GIVEN this concluding chapter the title it bears because the names of Borromini and Guarini cannot be left out of a consideration of the Italian attitude toward Gothic architecture in the seventeenth century. Before turning to them, however, I propose to switch back in time, so that we can see those great seventeenth-century masters in focus.

At the beginning of this book, I commented briefly on the intellectual break with the medieval past accomplished in fifteenth-century Italy. I now wish to add that, despite the gulf that progressive minds vividly felt between their own position and that of the recent past, at first one scarcely comes across any outspoken hostility against the *maniera tedesca* in architecture—in any case, not *expressis verbis*. So far as I know, no one voiced his disgust with the architectural past as vociferously as Vasari did in the mid-sixteenth century. Although Leon Battista Alberti laid the theoretical foundation of the classical

Renaissance doctrines, his various art-theoretical writings do not contain any strictures upon the barbaric arts of the past. There is no need to emphasize that his silence did not imply approval; but his broadmindedness is demonstrably visible at S. Maria Novella (fig. 4), at the Tempio Malatestiano in Rimini, and at the sensitive modernization of the Gothic Rucellai Chapel near that family's palace in Florence.

Filarete, whose treatise on architecture was written in the 1460s (shortly after Alberti's *Ten Books*), is fairly unique at that time in venting his detestation of Gothic architecture.[1] He expressed in words what many progressive people must have felt: "Praised be the memory of Brunelleschi who revived the architecture of the ancients. Therefore I beseech everyone to give up this modern (i.e., Gothic) habit of building, and do not let yourself be advised by those masters who make use of this bungling practice. Cursed be he who introduced it. I believe it was none other than barbarians who brought it to Italy."[2]

At the other pole there is such a figure as Filarete's contemporary, Aeneas Silvius Piccolomini (1405–64), a noted humanist and churchman who ascended the papal throne as Pius II in 1458. In this august position he immediately began to transform his birthplace Cosignano (by him renamed Pienza) near Arezzo in Tuscany into a showpiece of Renaissance architecture. But for the church which his architect Bernardo Rossellino built in accordance with the Pope's directives, a German Late Gothic hall type was used which has three naves of equal height (fig. 124). In the Pope's own words: "Thus Pius commanded it, who had seen this type among the Germans in Austria. This arrangement is more beautiful [than others] and makes the church lighter."[3] Aeneas Silvius combined a complete dedication to the new art of the Renaissance with an admiration for the Gothic style: he appreciated the beauty and splendor of the Gothic churches at Nuremberg as much as that of the great cathedral at Strasbourg.

When discussing the *Tiburio* of Milan Cathedral, we found that in the late 1480s and early 1490s Bramante and Leonardo themselves, moved by the principle of conformity, displayed a rather liberal attitude toward the *maniera tedesca*. Even the report on ancient and modern architecture, the antiquities of Rome and their preservation, written in the second decade of the sixteenth century and now usually and probably correctly attributed to Raphael—even this report, which contains a survey of the history of architecture, is not entirely hostile to the Gothic style. Raphael naturally links the rise of the German manner with a general decline of the arts. "That manner [he writes] is very far removed from the beautiful manner of the Romans and ancients. The Germans, whose style still survives in many places, often use as ornaments a little crouching figure, poorly executed [he is surely thinking of gargoyles], or strange animals, figures and leaves, all done without proper reason. Nevertheless [he continues] this architecture did make some sense, as it was derived from trees, not yet trimmed down, the branches of which were bent over and made to form pointed arches when tied together."[4] This idea arose, of course, as a counterpart to the Vitruvian legend of the origin of the Doric style from primitive wooden structures (fig. 126). Although, in Raphael's opinion, the rational antique method was vastly superior, the pedigree of the German manner was not wholly to be despised. In the eyes of men like Raphael the saving grace of the *maniera tedesca* was probably the notion that Greek and German architecture had one thing in common: they were both imitative arts derived from nature.

As the sixteenth century progressed, the theoretical position hardened, and at the mid-century mark Vasari's dislike of all things Gothic manifested a climax of negative reaction. Advanced architects of the second half of the century experimented with various facets of a strictly classical style: to cite but a few, Sanmicheli, Alessi, Vignola, and Palladio. Of these great architects only Vignola and Palladio made an occasional and, surprisingly, rather conciliatory remark about Gothic architecture. In his controversy with Ranuzzi about the façade design for S. Petronio, we have seen that Vignola noted, rather apologetically, that at the time of the original façade design, "good architecture had not yet been brought to light again, as it has in our century."[5] And Palladio expressed his respect for some Gothic buildings such as the Palazzo del Comune at Padua, the largest hall in the whole of Europe, as he believed. We have also noted that closer to the end of the century such an uncompromising classicist as Pellegrino Pellegrini advocated the continuation of the façade of S. Petronio in the Gothic manner rather than the mixing of incompatible styles. From all this (and I do not doubt that more examples could be given) one carries away the impression that even inveterate sixteenth-century classicists did not quite share Vasari's feeling of repugnance in front of a Gothic building. There is, indeed, at the turn of the sixteenth to the seventeenth century one architect who does not seem to fit this pattern, namely Vincenzo Scamozzi. He was born in 1552 and, after Palladio's death in 1580, he advanced to the position of the leading Venetian master. In the early years of the seventeenth century he enjoyed an international reputation that was buttressed by his bulky treatise, the *Idea dell'Architettura Universale*, published shortly before his death in 1615.[6] Scamozzi has a number of exceptionally important buildings to his credit and some of them, such as the Villa Pisani at Lonigo (near Vicenza), radiate an austere beauty and even charm, which, however, does not prevent us from feeling that his classicism was rather contrived and academic and that his intellectualism outshone his natural artistic endowment and his spontaneity.

The first book of his long treatise also contains a history of architecture from the point of view of an inflexible classicist, and here we find, of course, what we would expect.[7] When the Roman Empire fell prey to barbaric invasions, not only freedom disappeared, but also learning and the arts sank to a low level and for many centuries the true and good architecture was despised. He enlarges on this topic with examples, and this also leads him to Milan Cathedral. First he gives an idea of its impressive size, the nobility of the marble used, and the decoration with innumerable statues—but since this building is deficient in beauty of invention and universality of form, since, moreover, it lacks the right kind of proportional relationships between single members, nothing remains but a perforated (*traforato*) marble pile, a confused mass without any inner rule and law. This is the reason, he concludes, why the façade and other parts have remained unfinished.

About the palace of the Doges in Venice he says that an enormous body is being carried by weak shafts of columns, and he calls the palace deformed and ugly. In the same category belong the medieval basilicas at Padua and Vicenza and an infinity of other buildings in Italy. All this happened, Scamozzi argues, because at the time these buildings were erected there existed no real architects but only stupid handymen who worked without knowledge, guided merely by natural instinct, and so what they did approaches the ridiculous and monstrous.

But unexpectedly, there was also another side to Scamozzi, revealing a man who was much less dogmatic and who approached everything he saw with an open mind. Scamozzi was widely traveled. In the summer of 1599 he had accompanied the Venetian ambassador to the court of the King of Poland through Hungary, Bohemia, Germany, and France to Paris, where he arrived in mid-February 1600. A month later he left Paris in the retinue of another Venetian ambassador and returned to Venice. By a piece of good luck the diary Scamozzi wrote on this journey home survives (it is now in the Museo Civico at Vicenza), and a few years ago this little treasure was very well published by Franco Barbieri (fig. 125).[8] It opened up entirely new perspectives regarding Scamozzi. His journey took him via St.

Denis along the Marne, where he stopped at Meaux and Châlons-sur-Marne. From there he went to Toul, Nancy, St.-Nicolas-de-Port, and on to Basel, and then through Switzerland to Locarno and along the Lago Maggiore into Italy. The comments he jotted down during the journey are lively and observant, but what is of the greatest interest to us is that he was attracted by many of the Gothic churches he saw on the way. Often he briefly put down his reaction to them and, what is more, he found them interesting enough to sketch them when he had a chance. These sketches were, of course, not more than rough annotations, but although we catch him making a great many trifling errors, he was remarkably accurate as far as the major motifs were concerned.

The church of St. Denis he called a most noble structure and filled a sheet with its plan, façade, elevation, and several details (figs. 127, 128). He even took time to chart the most important measurements. The façade, badly restored in the nineteenth century, lost its north tower in 1846–47. Scamozzi shows the façade, by and large correctly, in its original condition. The essential features of the façade of the cathedral at Meaux he also caught extremely well (figs. 129, 130). He says of this church that it is of considerable beauty. The cathedral at Toul attracted him so much that he drew it rather carefully and gave a detailed description of it (fig. 131). It is perhaps strange that he described St.-Nicolas-de-Port as particularly beautiful, for the church has a very distinct irregularity: midway the plan shows a twist towards a more southerly direction (fig. 133). Scamozzi's sketches of the plan and façade of this church help us to understand how he saw such buildings: *his* plan of the church is absolutely straight (fig. 132), and in his imagination also the façade consisted of entirely regular horizontals and verticals and a perfectly balanced disposition of motifs.

Nevertheless, even though Scamozzi may have seen such buildings with the eyes and mind of a sworn classicist, they belonged to the accursed barbaric *maniera tedesca* about which he had such harsh things to say when he addressed an international public in his book. I would not want to pronounce ex cathedra that Scamozzi was talking with two tongues nor that he had a dual standard of values, a private and a public one. In all likelihood he was scarcely or even not at all aware of his inconsistency. In any case, we are faced here with an ambivalence similar to Vasari's and we can and, I think, *must* conclude that the doors were never entirely closed to an appreciation of individual Gothic buildings, even at the moment of the strictest classical dogmatism—provided, of course, that no violation of principle was involved. When that happened, the iron curtain fell: it was the appeal to, and belief in, the supreme power of reason that precluded any pact with the irrationality of Gothic conventions and taste.

When Scamozzi died in Venice at age 64 in July 1616, a young man by the name of Borromini, then seventeen years old, was growing up in Milan in the architectural climate of the post-Pellegrini era, which was not too far removed from Scamozzi's Venetian legacy. Borromini was born into a family of stonemasons at Bissone on the Lake of Lugano, an area that had supplied Italy with stonemasons and architects for generations. His father apprenticed him, still a boy, in Milan and it may be assumed that he worked there for almost a decade (i.e., from about 1610 to 1619) before making his way to Rome. Nothing at all is known about his early Milanese years, but there are indications that they had a formative influence on him, an influence of greater importance than has generally been realized. It is well known that upon his arrival in Rome he was first engaged as a stonemason in St. Peter's (fig. 134) and that it took some years for him to advance to the position of architect under his kinsman, the then papal architect Carlo Maderno.

So, Borromini was certainly trained as a stonemason in Milan, and it is reasonable to assume that he belonged to the army of stonemasons constantly needed by the cathedral. The cathedral documents teach us that on the level of stonemasons' work, Gothic detail was carried out all the time virtually without interruption through the seventeenth and eighteenth centuries. We may therefore take it that Borromini most likely did some Gothic work himself in these early years and imbibed the medieval masons' traditions. If I am now attacked for having fallen victim to fanciful speculations, my protective armor could easily be pierced, but I can claim two facts in my defense: first, Borromini's architectural work in Rome shows that he was conversant with Gothic conventions, and secondly, even if he was never given a mason's job in the cathedral, the overwhelming presence of the enormous building and its problems—to which all Milanese were alive—would have conditioned him to an understanding of, and an interest in, Gothic structural traditions.

The fact that in Rome Borromini was a kind of outsider who had brought Gothic tendencies along from Milan was not hidden from his contemporaries. Thus Monsignor Cartari, a learned librarian whose remarkably well-informed diary has only recently come to light,[9] reports that on the occasion of a visit to Borromini's church of S. Ivo (fig. 136) the Chigi Pope Alexander VII stated: "The style of

Cavalier Borromini was Gothic, nor is this surprising, since he was born in Milan where the cathedral is Gothic." Other observations of this kind were made during Borromini's lifetime. When Bernini was in Paris in 1665 Frenchmen discussed Borromini, as we are informed in the Sieur de Chantelou's diary. Borromini's architecture was called bizarre and chimerical; in the context in which these remarks were made, they were apparently aimed at his medievalizing and at other vagaries and were meant to censure him for not accepting classical anthropometry (i.e., man and his measurements) as the standard and focus of his architecture. Finally, Giovanni Bellori, the mid-seventeenth-century mouthpiece of classical orthodoxy, coined the notorious phrase about S. Carlo alle Quattro Fontane (fig. 135) that this church's architecture was ugly and deformed and its architect was a Gothic ignoramus and one who corrupted architecture ("un gotico ignorantissimo e corruttore dell'-architettura").

We see, therefore, that Borromini's medievalism is not a modern discovery: On the contrary, it excited his contemporaries more than it does many of us, though the tracing of medieval motifs in Borromini's architecture has lately become quite an art-historical game. I would like to point out in particular the combination of two shapes in the mighty pediment of Borromini's façade of the Oratory of St. Philip Neri (fig. 137), a pediment usually regarded as a characteristically Borrominesque and, at the same time, typically Baroque extravaganza, but one which is in reality a reinterpretation of the late-medieval crowning motif of the façade of Milan's old cathedral of S. Maria Maggiore, a façade that remained standing inside the new cathedral through most of the seventeenth century (fig. 16). While the connection is patently obvious, one would then have to deal with the motif, with how he integrated the movement in the pediment with the concepts of structural energy animating the entire façade.

There are many other remarkable connections with Milan Cathedral and with traditional medieval motifs in Borromini's work. Not wanting to give overwhelming details, let me at least point out such features as the angular intersection of moldings over the doors inside Borromini's greatest church, S. Ivo della Sapienza, so obviously opposed to the classical manner of framing doors, but in keeping with a Late Gothic tradition (fig. 138). Or take such an isolated plastic shape as the lavabo in the Oratory of St. Philip Neri (fig. 139), which has no counterpart in Renaissance or baroque art and which most people would therefore have great difficulties in dating correctly: the base is clearly fashioned after similar Late Gothic lavabos, while the huge opening blossom crowning the base seems to anticipate (as Dagobert Frey wrote fifty years ago[10]) the early-nineteenth-century neo-Gothic creations of Percier and Fontaine. This verdict is, however, not fully acceptable, for the blossom has, as it were, a built-in spring, an astonishingly lively quality, far removed from neo-Gothic dehydrated designs.

Instead of increasing the list of individual Gothic features let us turn to two more essential medievalizing aspects of Borromini's style. First, if I am not mistaken, Borromini brought along with him from Milan the mason's tradition of medieval geometry and never abandoned this tradition in favor of the Renaissance-Baroque procedure, derived from Vitruvius, of planning solely in terms of modules, i.e., in terms of a basic unit such as the diameter of the column, its multiplication and division. Fortunately, a number of preparatory drawings by Borromini survive which leave no doubt about his procedure. In studying a preparatory drawing for S. Carlo alle Quattro Fontane, Borromini's first church, built between 1638 and 1641 (fig. 140), we make the strange discovery that this extraordinary spatial creation was controlled by triangulation (fig. 141). The lozenge-shaped parallelogram, the basic geometrical figure used here, consists of two equilateral triangles with a common base. The prependiculars erected over each of the four sides of the parallelogram determine the position of the chapels. At the same time, the perpendiculars form a second configuration of two equilateral triangles whose perpendiculars correspond to half a side of the primary triangles. This is pure medieval geometry. In his 1521 edition of Vitruvius, Cesariano had published the plan of Milan Cathedral and here we find that the cathedral's length and width were determined by two equilateral triangles with a common base (figs. 26, 27).

Let me give another slightly more complicated example from Borromini's late period. When he died in 1667 the dome of S. Andrea delle Fratte was left a magnificent fragment in raw brick (fig. 144). This drumlike feature was to be crowned by a lantern with concave recesses over the convex walls underneath. There is a drawing in the Albertina in Vienna (where most Borromini drawings are to be found) showing a ground plan of the lantern drawn into a plan of the drum underneath (fig. 142). When you look closely at this rather complicated drawing, you will find that everything falls comparatively easily into place (fig. 143). It appears that the shape of the lantern is geometrically derived from, and geometrically determined by, the design of the drum, and it is this—the geometrical unification of different stories shown in one and the same ground plan (fig. 142)—that reveals the closest contact with late-medieval principles.

Now on to the second medievalizing aspect under discussion. The central problem of Italian ecclesiastical architecture of the Renaissance and Baroque periods was the great vault of the dome, the symbolic image of heaven—epitomized in Michelangelo's dome of St. Peter's and the many domes depending on it. Circumstances forced Borromini to build one dome in this tradition, namely S. Agnese in Piazza Navona, when he was independent, however—as in S. Carlo alle Quattro Fontane and in S. Ivo—he broke away from the customary central-Italian rising curve of the dome and encased it, following an old North-Italian tradition. But it is even more interesting that already in his middle period a tendency to abandon domical features altogether becomes noticeable. The most telling and most accomplished example of this tendency is the church he built in the Collegio di Propaganda Fide in the 1660s, shortly before his death (figs. 145, 146). Here an order of monumental pilasters rhythmically accentuates the entire perimeter of the space, a rectangle with rounded-off corners. The pilasters produce a strong vertical effect that is continued through the projecting entablature into the bands crisscrossing diagonally the relatively flat vault. An unbroken system closely ties together all parts of the building in all directions. In contrast to the broad stream of the Italian tradition according to which, as in Roman architecture, the wall forms a constituent and active element of the building, we are faced here with what might be termed a skeleton structure in a true sense; for piers and ribs, one imagines, could form a coherent, stable skeleton even if the small pieces of wall between them were removed. This is indeed a Gothic structural system: no post-Renaissance building in Italy had come so close to Gothic structural principles. It is now also clear that in such a system there was no place for a traditional type of dome.

This would seem an appropriate moment to turn from Borromini to Guarini, but before leaving Borromini I feel it should be emphasized that his leaning toward Gothic principles was neither eclectic nor historicizing nor romantic (as has sometimes been said). It may be regarded as the rediscovery of a treasured architectural language to which he felt drawn by a deep-rooted affinity and which his genius was capable of adapting to the classical syntax of forms (such as orders, entablatures, classical moldings, and so forth) without which he, a man of his age and the great pioneer of unconventional architectural thinking, could not envisage a building. Regrettably, Borromini kept posterity guessing as to what was going on in his mind. There is not a word by him that would reveal his own ideas about Gothic architecture. By contrast, Guarini was more communicative.

Guarini was twenty-five years younger than Borromini. Born at Modena in 1624, he entered the Order of the Theatines as a boy of fifteen. He studied theology, philosophy, mathematics, and architecture in Rome. He was immensely richly endowed by nature not only as an architect but also as an intellect capable of rare power of penetration.[11] He began his career as a teacher of philosophy and mathematics at Messina in Sicily and henceforth published important books on philosophy, mathematics, fortification, and, when he died in 1683, had an architectural treatise almost ready for the press. Its publication was, however, delayed by more than half a century. Eventually, the Theatines handed all the material over to Bernardo Vittone, who brought the book out in 1737.[12] Guarini's most active and creative years as a designer were the last seventeen of his life, which he spent as court architect to the house of Savoy at Turin (figs. 147, 148). We are well informed about this period, and his Turinese buildings testify to the greatness as well as the strangeness of his architectural conceptions. But we have to turn to his treatise for an exposition of many of his ideas, among them his thoughts on Gothic architecture.

Guarini's treatise contains more references to Gothic architecture than any architectural treatise before his. These passages show that Gothic buildings gave him much food for thought, and while he does not offer a watertight theory, many of his observations are surprising and of the utmost interest. At the end of his discussion of the architectural orders, he has a chapter on the Gothic Order and its proportion (fig. 149).[13] This theme is introduced by some general observations. They contain the following points: The Goths were at first out to destroy rather than to build, but the Mediterranean nations—Spaniards, French, and Italians—tamed them and turned the former destroyers into ingenious builders. As proof of this contention he enumerates such skillful structures as the churches at Seville and Salamanca, the cathedrals of Reims and Paris, Milan Cathedral, the Certosa of Pavia, S. Petronio at Bologna, and Siena Cathedral. This kind of architecture, he informs his readers, was erected without stable rules, on the basis of workshop practice handed down from father to son. The Goths liked elongated proportions, gave their columns excessive heights, and in order not to sacrifice the slenderness of which they were so fond they joined together a number of thin columns and thus created a compound column. Their aims, he continues, were totally opposed to those of the Roman architects. And now follows a most remarkable passage. In contrast to the qualities of strength and solidity aimed at by Roman architects, Gothic builders wanted their churches to appear structurally weak so it should seem miraculous that they could stand up at all. In his words, Gothic builders erected arches "which seem to hang in the air; completely perforated towers crowned by pointed pyramids; enormously high windows and vaults without the support of walls. The corner of a high tower may rest on an arch or a column or on the apex of a vault," and the passage ends with the words: "Which of the two opposing methods, the Roman or the Gothic, is the more wonderful, would be a nice problem for an academic mind."

More than a hundred years before Guarini, Vasari had analyzed the Gothic style, and Scamozzi's sallies were written about seventy years before. Indeed, much had happened. In historical perspective it would seem that the mid-seventeenth-century events concerning the façade of Milan Cathedral, events that had the widest intra-Italian repercussions, prepared the ground for Guarini's appreciation of Gothic architecture. But we must also consider that his analysis of this style contains a good deal of self-revelation. The elements of surprise and of the miraculous which he discovered in Gothic architecture belong essentially to his own style (figs. 151, 153). And when he conceived the principles of his diaphanous domes, which seem to defy all laws of statics, he may have found support in the principles that, according to him, ruled Gothic architecture.

Two more passages, which are most revealing for the changing intellectual climate during the later seventeenth century, may find a place here. Guarini comments on the relativity of taste. A terse sentence simply states: "First the Goths disliked Roman architecture, and now we dislike Gothic architecture." In a similar vein he argues that even ideas on proportion are dependent on changing customs and interest. There were times, he says, when Gothic architecture was found pleasing, and yet today it is not only disliked but even derided. If, however, one considers Gothic architecture without prejudice, one is bound to admit that ingenious men erected splendid buildings—buildings that are truly miraculous and worthy of high praise.[14]

Clearly, Guarini was infatuated with Gothic buildings, and an echo of his theoretical considerations may (as I have indicated) be found in his architectural practice. But in actual fact, not one of his buildings looks Gothic; they only evoke principles realized by the ingenious Gothic builders rather than by the masters of the Renaissance. Thus it is by analogy and association and hence in a symbolic, not in a straightforward positivist sense that a relationship between

Guarini's structures—especially his domes and Gothic building conventions—is revealed.

But there is yet another aspect to Guarini's Gothicism. Between 1662 and 1665 Guarini was in Paris, building there for his Order the church Sainte-Anne-la-Royale (figs. 150, 152) and during this period he acquired an intimate knowledge of recent French advances in the field of geometry. The concern of these mathematical scholars was the plane projection of spherical surfaces and the transformation of plane surfaces of a given shape into corresponding surfaces of a different shape. A lengthy section of Guarini's treatise is devoted to these matters and in the introduction to this part he declared that a knowledge of such operations was absolutely necessary to the architect; that the Italians scarcely knew about them but that the French had done splendid work in the field. For, he carries on, in order to be able to cut stones along the correct sections and to have a precise knowledge of their surfaces this science is necessary. A fair number of plates of Guarini's treatise illustrate this kind of operation (figs. 154, 155). The key phrase in Guarini's text is the reference to the cutting of stones, for this indicates that Guarini was familiar with a branch of literature very much at home in France and called by the French "La coupe des pierres."

The science of the section of solids, such as stones, walls, ceilings, and vaults, is called stereotomy, and there exists now a rapidly growing art-historical literature on these matters, mainly owing to the work of a historian of science, Werner Müller, who has closely investigated Guarini's contribution to this field, and, moreover, a young Italian architectural historian, Paolo Marconi, has correctly pointed out that the men who produced the literature on stereotomy in the seventeenth century in France (figs. 156, 157) were primarily Jesuits (among them Father François Derand is the most important one) and that the same Jesuits brought about a seventeenth-century Gothic revival in France.[15] Stereotomy was now needed in order to be able to construct the vaults of the new Gothic churches. Thus in the context of stereotomy Guarini's Gothicism would seem to merge with a return to carefully studied Gothic methods of construction in seventeenth-century France. I do not want to conclude the subject of Guarini and the Gothic style without at least a passing reference to a strange man, Caramuel, who must be regarded as a fairly recent art-historical discovery.

Juan Caramuel de Lobkowitz, a Spanish nobleman born in Madrid in 1606, was a mathematician, astronomer, theologian, diplomatist, soldier, and architect. This paragon of a seventeenth-century scholar, who is reputed to have known more than twenty languages, spent the last ten years of his life as Bishop of Vigevano in Lombardy. He published an endless number of books on every topic under the sun, but only his architectural treatise, brought out in 1678,[16] is of interest here. A hundred years later the neo-classicist Leopoldo Cicognara called Caramuel's book "an undigested collection of everything known about architecture." Guarini often quotes Caramuel, usually to attack him vigorously, especially his so-called "architettura interest here is that Caramuel was immensely taken by Gothic archi- obliqua," a prickly topic which I cannot discuss here. What is of tecture. There are, in fact, so many parallels between Caramuel's and Guarini's texts, that we are bound to assume that Guarini was stimulated by Caramuel with regard to matters concerning the Gothic style.

The pervasive influence of both Borromini and Guarini upon later generations of architects is well known and has become a topic of steadily increasing academic studies in the last thirty or forty years. My concern is to inquire very briefly into the effect that Borromini's and Guarini's opening-up toward Gothic buildings had on their successors. This question is not easily answered, but it seems legitimate to say that we would seek in vain for manifest signs of a growing interest in Gothic architecture as we turn from the seventeenth to the eighteenth century. We have to realize that at this time Italian architectural theory declined in importance and breadth of vision; and we have to acknowledge that in this respect Italy had yielded supremacy to France already in the seventeenth century. As the eighteenth century advanced, English theory superseded French theory. It is indicative of this fundamental change in the intellectual relationships between European nations that Francesco Milizia, Italy's foremost neo-classical theoretician, based large sections of his *Principles of Civic Architecture* (published in 1781) on Sir William Chambers's *Treatise of Civil Architecture* (of 1759). This, incidentally, is not my discovery, but that of a former Columbia student, Etta Arntzen.

One cannot claim that in the wake of Borromini and Guarini Italian architectural practice was inclining toward a revival of Gothic tendencies. We cannot find any Italian parallels to, say, Hawksmore's English neo-Gothic experiments shortly after 1700 (figs. 158, 159). It is also characteristic that the vigorous and rich development of the neo-Gothic movement in the later eighteenth century in Italy brought what I would like to call crypto-Gothic tendencies to fruition which were indeed stimulated by the examples of the two great seventeenth-century masters.

AFTERWORD

T HESE WORDS MARK the end of this intriguing and previously almost unknown story, and of Rudolf Wittkower's manuscript, which we his students and colleagues read for the Mathews lecture series as his surrogates. Because it is a somewhat abrupt end, I should like to attempt a summing up that he planned and even wrote, but which has not been found.

Professor Wittkower must have wished to reflect on the significance of an age bemused by its descent from two quite different cultures—a grandparent culture of the Greeks and Romans that was human scaled and subject to well-defined laws, and a parent culture which Italians always felt had been imposed on them by northerners, especially Germans, that was supernatural and somewhat irrational in spite of its logical and mathematical apparatus. The period of the thirteenth and fourteenth centuries in Italy was a time of great city growth as well as of church-building fervor, and the two combined in the foundation of the great cathedrals in the style of the moment, Gothic. Not long after came the fresh surge of enthusiasm for the achievements of the ancient world that we know as the Renaissance, and medieval things, when not despised, were felt to be old-fashioned and lacking in the superior virtues of the surviving arts, letters, history, and philosophy of the ancients. Meanwhile, those grandiose urban cathedrals were still being built, and—since churches are always started at the altar end so they could be used during construction—in every case (except Siena) what was lacking was a proper façade. The facade, or more precisely its decorative veneer, though of minor importance for the functioning of the building, was of great symbolic moment, being the showpiece of the commune and of the church as an institution. That is why the controversies between proponents of the ancient and the medieval style raged with such intensity over cathedral façades, and why they rarely could be resolved before the 1800s, when both traditions seemed remote enough to permit them to be elected at will or even combined in a single work.

What the present study reveals that would not have been expected is that the controversy was never between lovers of antiquity and lovers of the middle ages—that dialectic was an eighteenth-century diversion. The protagonists were rather two kinds of classicists. Wherever the confrontation occurred, one party claimed that since the Roman style represented reason, and the Gothic fantasy, the Roman should be preferred regardless of the particular conditions. The other claimed that the principles of concordance (Alberti's *concinnitas*) and propriety (Vitruvius' *decorum*) demanded that a building be of one style, and the fact that the style was Gothic did not justify departures from the principles. The rationale of the latter argument was drawn originally from Roman texts on rhetoric and oratory which were exacting on matters of style, and which had been the single most important catalyst in the formation of the humanist aesthetic of the early Renaissance.

Considering how many voices were raised against the Gothic in the centuries of the Renaissance, we are fortunate that so many medieval churches were preserved. But not fortunate enough to see the interiors of many of them as they were originally conceived; the romanizing spirit and later purisms led to the removal of the choir walls and screens that so often crossed the naves, and to the replacement of the old tombs and tabernacles along the walls by Renaissance and Baroque monuments.

But we have seen in chapter five how, because the churches survived, the ground was prepared for the ultimate fusion of the Gothic and the Roman styles in the Baroque imagination of Borromini and Guarini, who in different ways had come into close contact with medieval building traditions.

The lectures from which this book is compiled are an apt finale to the richly productive career of a beloved master scholar and teacher of so many younger Britons and Americans; more than any other student of architecture he had been concerned with the impact of the classical tradition on Renaissance and Baroque design. He will be remembered for many bequests of learning to posterity, and most of all for two achievements: first, the uncountable number of important artists, architects, buildings, sculptures, and designs which he drew from obscurity into the light, documented, and interpreted, and second, the clarification of the major architectural theories and controversies in the three centuries from Alberti to the Enlightenment. This study of the Gothic during those centuries gives a new dimension to its predecessors by applying the methods developed by the author to an account of the classical tradition as it encountered its only serious competition.

JAMES S. ACKERMAN

1. Orvieto Cathedral. Detail of façade. 14th century.

2. Orvieto Cathedral. Detail of façade.

3. Vasari. Frame for 14th-century "Cimabue" drawing.

4. Florence. S. Maria Novella.

5. Milan. Piazza and cathedral.

6. Milan Cathedral. The *Tiburio*.

7. Milan. Interior of cathedral.

8. Milan Cathedral. Tracery work; left: old pinnacles, right: pinnacles of 1927.

9. Milan Cathedral. Section of the *Tiburio* as built. Engraving.

10. Milan. Plan showing building site with old S. Maria Maggiore (3), Palazzo Ducale (5), and new cathedral as planned in 1389.

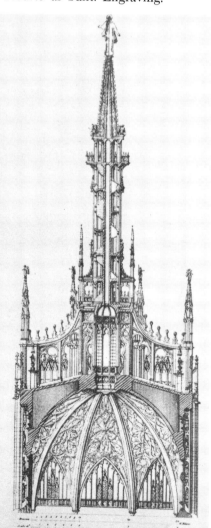

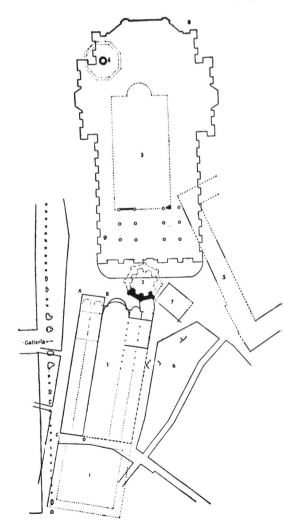

11. Milan. Site of cathedral and neighboring buildings. 17th century.

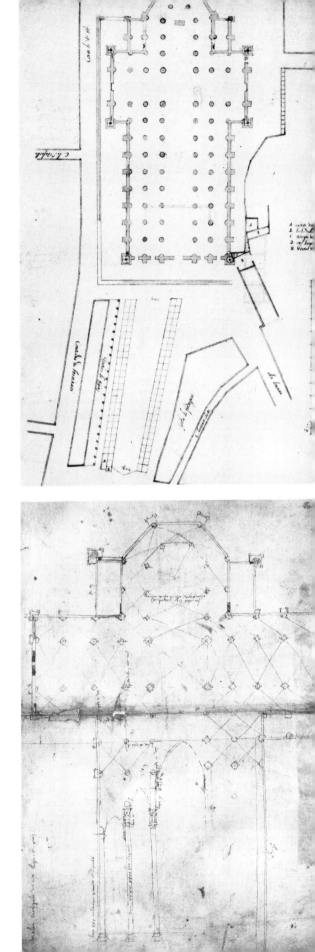

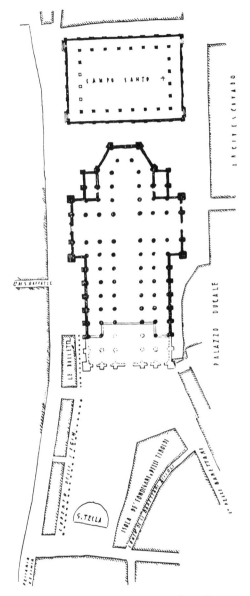

12. Milan. Plan of cathedral. Mid-16th century.

13. Antonio di Vincenzo. Sketch after the designs for Milan Cathedral. 1390.

14. Milan Cathedral. Unfinished façade and *Tiburio*. Engraving. 1633.

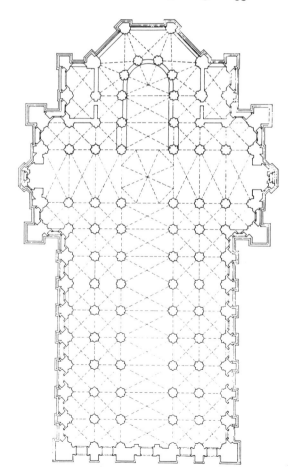

15. Milan Cathedral.
Plan of the present building.

16. Milan. Stone relief showing façade of old S. Maria Maggiore.

17. Melchiorre Gherardoni. Piazza and façade of Milan Cathedral at the time of the funeral of Cardinal Cesare Monti. 1650. Engraving.

18. Milan Cathedral. State of the façade in 1683. Anonymous painting, showing old S. Maria Maggiore inside the new structure.

19. Milan Cathedral. Aspect of the façade at the time of the funeral of the Queen of Sardinia. 1735. Engraving.

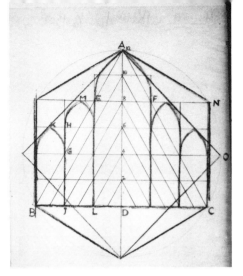

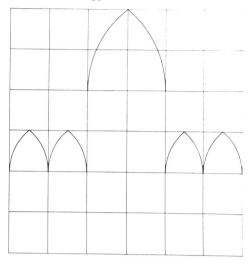

21. Milan Cathedral. Cross section *ad quadratum* according to Heinrich Parler. 1392.

20. Stornaloco's triangulated proposal for the cross section of Milan Cathedral (1391) with a circle, square, and hexagon superimposed to illustrate the geometric figures on which his proportions were based.

22. Milan Cathedral. Left: System as accepted by the Fabbrica in 1392 with Pythagorean triangulation for upper nave. Right: Stornaloco's system as in fig. 20. (after Beltrami)

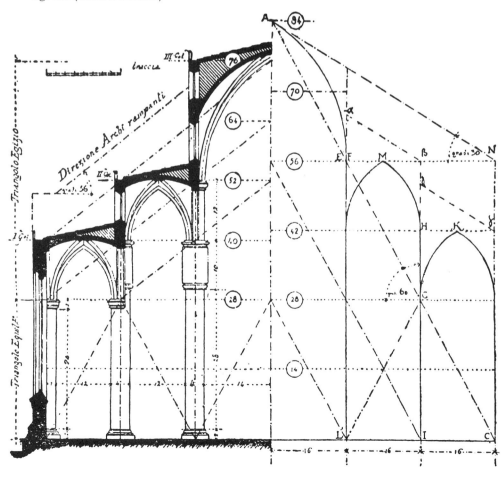

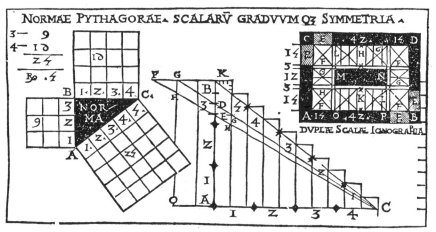

23. Cesare Cesariano. *Vitruvius.* 1521. Pythagorean triangle.

24. Cesare Cesariano. Illustration for *Vitruvius,* book I, chapter II, showing the geometrical system of Milan Cathedral.

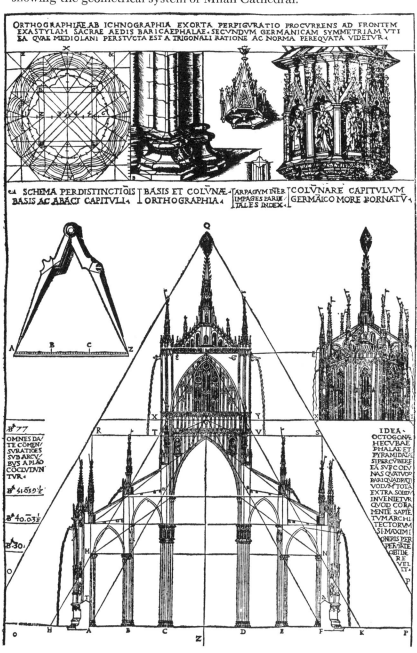

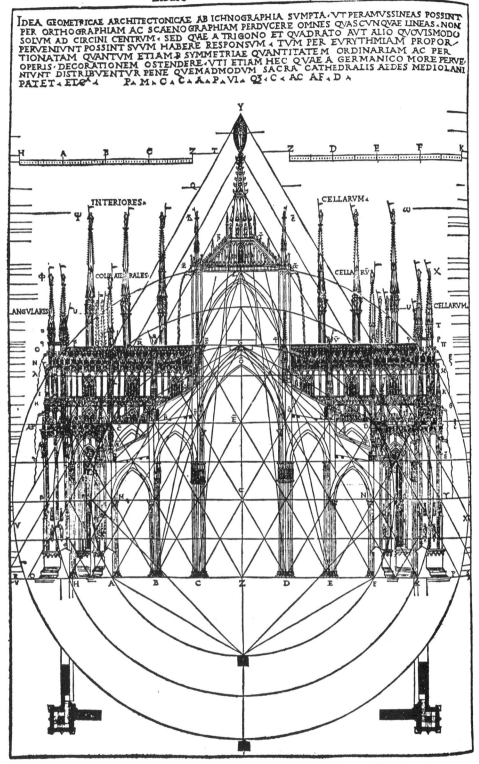

IDEA GEOMETRICAE ARCHITECTONICAE AB ICHNOGRAPHIA SVMPTA VT PERAMVSSINEAS POSSINT
PER ORTHOGRAPHIAM AC SCAENOGRAPHIAM PERDVCERE OMNES QVASCVNQVAE LINEAS NON
SOLVM AD CIRCINI CENTRVM SED QVAE A TRIGONO ET QVADRATO AVT ALIO QVOVISMODO
PERVENIVNT POSSINT SVVM HABERE RESPONSVM TVM PER EVRYTHMIAM PROPOR
TIONATAM QVANTVM ETIAM & SYMMETRIAE QVANTITATEM ORDINARIAM AC PER
OPERIS DECORATIONEM OSTENDERE VTI ETIAM HEC QVAE A GERMANICO MORE PERVE
NIVNT DISTRIBVENTVR PENE QVEMADMODVM SACRA CATHEDRALIS AEDES MEDIOLANI
PATET ETC. P M C A A P VI Q3 C AC AF D

25. Cesare Cesariano. Illustration for *Vitruvius*, book I, chapter II, showing Milan Cathedral *ad quadratum*, *ad triangulum*, and *ad circulum*. Compare fig. 20.

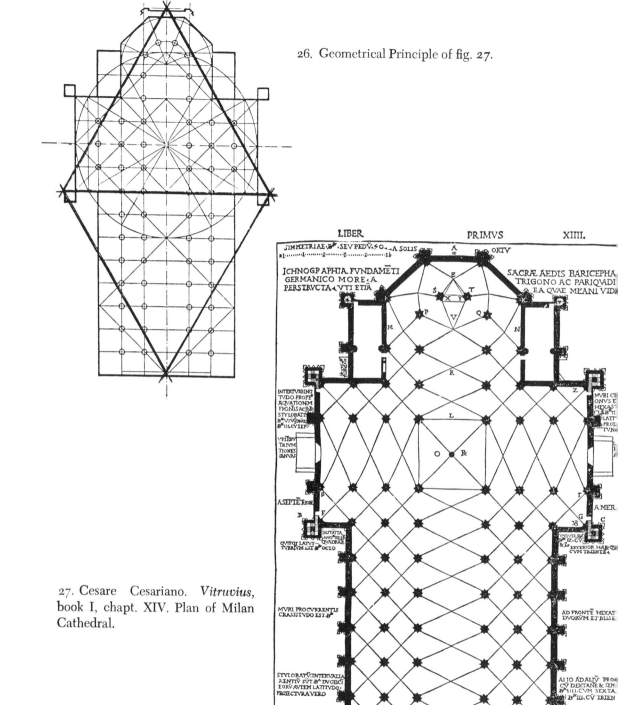

26. Geometrical Principle of fig. 27.

27. Cesare Cesariano. *Vitruvius*, book I, chapt. XIV. Plan of Milan Cathedral.

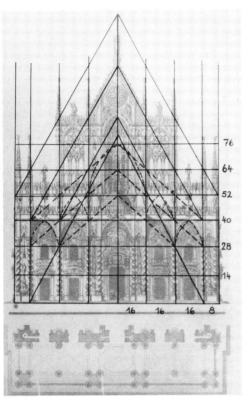

28. Luigi Vanvitelli. Project for Façade of Milan Cathedral (see fig. 73) with superimposed geometrical system as drawn by Karl Noehles.

29. François Blondel. *Cours d'architecture*. 1683. Section of Milan Cathedral.

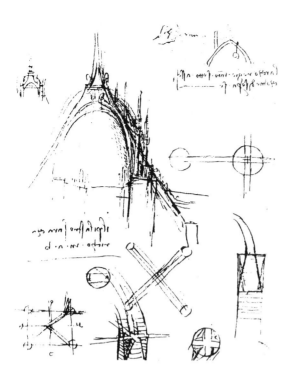

30. Leonardo da Vinci. Sketches for the *Tiburio*. Late 15th century.

31. Leonardo da Vinci. Sketches for the *Tiburio*.

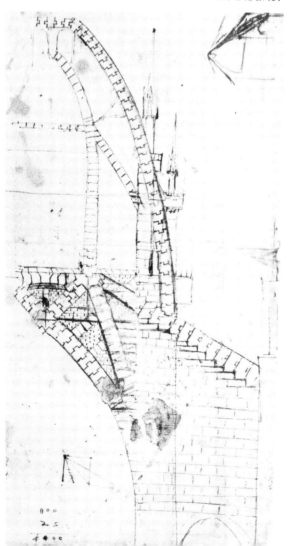

32. Vincenzo Seregni. Plan for Milan Cathedral. 1537. Drawing.

33. Vincenzo Seregni. Design for wall and portal of the north transept of Milan Cathedral. Between 1534 and 1537.

34. Vincenzo Seregni. Project for north transept of Milan Cathedral. After 1537. Woodcut.

35. Pellegrino Pellegrini (?). Design for the façade of Milan Cathedral.

36. Milan Cathedral. Façade. Engraved by Francesco Castelli in 1646 after the design by Pellegrino Pellegrini of *ca.* 1580.

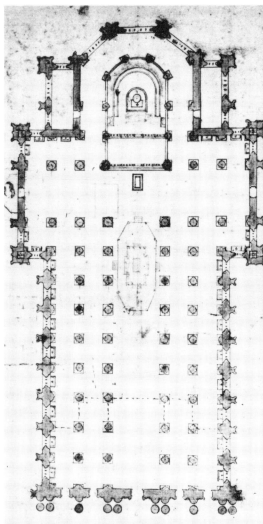

37. Pellegrini (?). Design for half
of the façade of Milan Cathedral.

38. Pellegrino Pellegrini (Studio?).
Plan for Milan Cathedral.

39. Martino Bassi. Design for the façade of Milan Cathedral. *Ca.* 1590.

40. Martino Bassi. Design for the façade of Milan Cathedral. *Ca.* 1590.

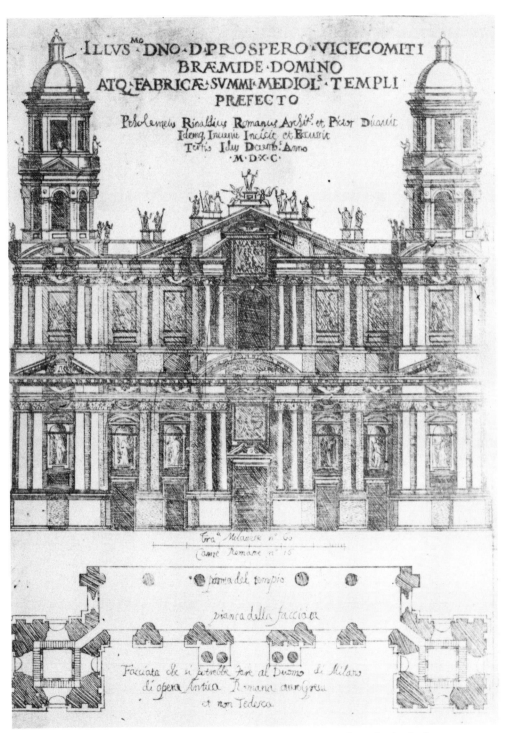

41. Tolomeo Rinaldi. Design for the façade of Milan Cathedral. 1590.
Engraving.

42. Carlo Maderno. S. Susanna, Rome. Façade.

43. Rome. St. Peter's. Detail of façade.

44. Francesco Maria Ricchino. Engraving of projects for the façade of
Milan Cathedral. 1635. Left half showing Pellegrini's design, right half with
Ricchino's alternative for upper tier.

45. Ricchino. Unfinished preparatory drawing for the engraving,
fig. 44.

46. Ricchino. Reinterpretation of
Pellegrini's design for the façade
of Milan Cathedral. Mirror image
added to left half of fig. 44.

47. Ricchino. Project for the façade of Milan Cathedral. Mirror image added to right half of fig. 44. Engraving. 1635.

48. Ricchino. Design for the façade of Milan Cathedral. 1603 (?).

49. Ricchino. Design for the façade of Milan Cathedral. 1606.

50. Ricchino. Two alternative suggestions for the façade of Milan Cathedral. 1610 (?).

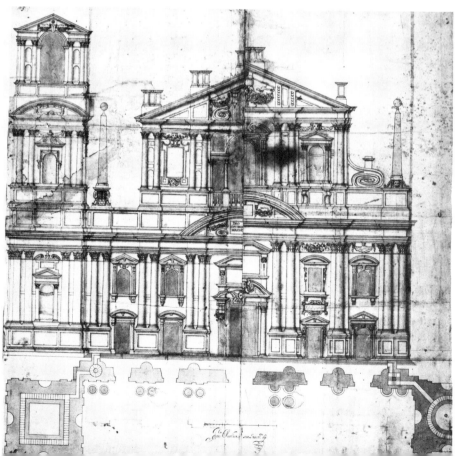

51. Ricchino. Project with towers for the façade of Milan Cathedral.
Center flap folded up. 1610 (?).

52. Ricchino. Project with towers for the façade of Milan Cathedral.
Same as fig. 51, but with center flap turned down.

53. Gerolamo da Sesto De Capitaneis. Design for the façade of
Milan Cathedral. 1608.

54. Giovan Paolo Bisnati. Drawing, showing side view of Milan Cathedral
in relation to the flank of Bisnati's design for the façade.

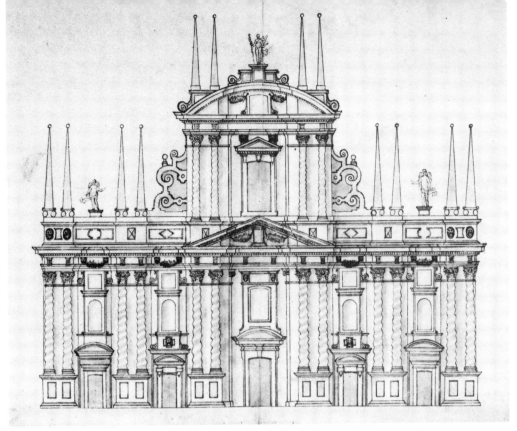

55. Anonymous design for the façade of Milan Cathedral.

56. Fabio Mangone. Project for the façade of Milan Cathedral. Engraving. See fig. 16.

57. Anonymous design for the façade of Milan Cathedral.

58. Lelio Buzzi or Lorenzo Bi-
nago(?). Design for the façade of
Milan Cathedral.

59. Anonymous design for the façade of Milan Cathedral. 18th century (?).

60. Carlo Buzzi. Design with Gothic windows for the façade of Milan Cathedral. 1653.

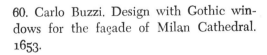

FACE de L'ÉGLISE de St AMBROISE qu'on Apelle le DOME de MILAN

Se Vend à AMSTERDAM chez P. MORTIER Avec Privilege.

61. Carlo Buzzi. Design with towers for the façade of Milan Cathedral. 1645 (?).

62. Carlo Buzzi. Design without towers for the façade of Milan Cathedral. 1645 (?). Engraving.

63. Carlo Buzzi. Flank of Milan Cathedral with Buzzi's towers as in fig. 61. Engraving.

64. Francesco Castelli. Design for the façade of Milan Cathedral. 1648.

65. Francesco Castelli. Section of façade of Milan Cathedral. Engraving.

66. Francesco Castelli. Side elevation with portico of Milan Cathedral.

67. Francesco Castelli. Second project for the façade of Milan Cathedral. 1651. Engraving.

68. Carlo Giuseppe Merlo. Design for the façade of Milan Cathedral with two alternative suggestions.

69. Anonymous. Design for the façade of Milan Cathedral.

70. Anonymous. Design for the façade of Milan Cathedral.

71. Anonymous. Design for the façade of Milan Cathedral.

72. Marco Bianco (?). Project for the façade of Milan Cathedral. After 1730 (?).

73. Luigi Vanvitelli. Design for the façade of Milan Cathedral. 1745. Compare with fig. 28.

74. Luigi Vanvitelli. Preparatory sketch for the design fig. 73.

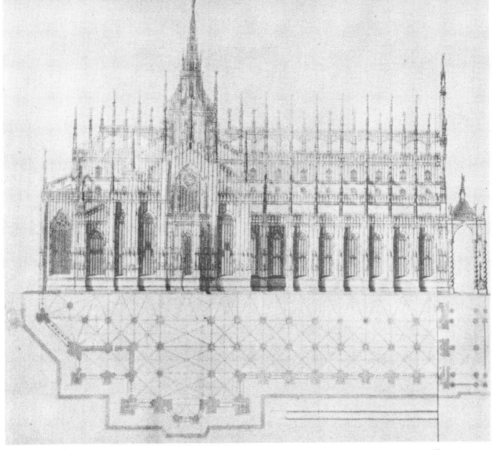

75. Carlo Giuseppe Merlo. Flank of Milan Cathedral with Vanvitelli s portico. See fig. 73.

76. Same, with side view of Merlo's own design of façade.

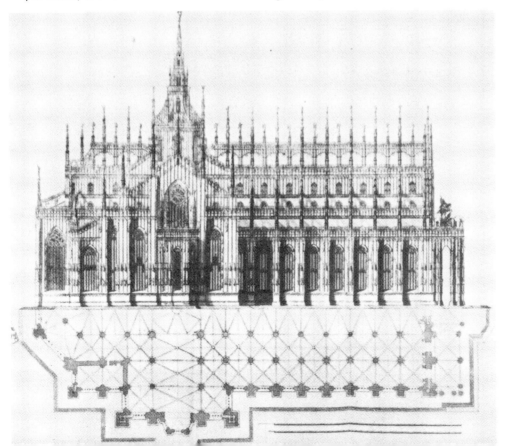

77. Antonio Maria Vertemate Cotognola. Design for the façade of Milan Cathedral. Frontal view and section.

78. Bernardo Vittone. Design for the façade of Milan Cathedral. 1746. Engraving.

79. Bernardo Vittone. S. Maria dell' Assunta. Grignasco. Design ca. 1749. Building begun after 1750. This church, characteristic of Vittone's style, dates from the same period as his "gothicizing" designs for Milan Cathedral.

80. Bernardo Vittone. Design for the façade of Milan Cathedral. 1746. Engraving.

81. Giulio Galliori. Design for the façade of Milan Cathedral. 1786-87.

82. Giovan Battista Riccardi. Design for the façade of Milan Cathedral. 1746. Portico not visible in ground plan.

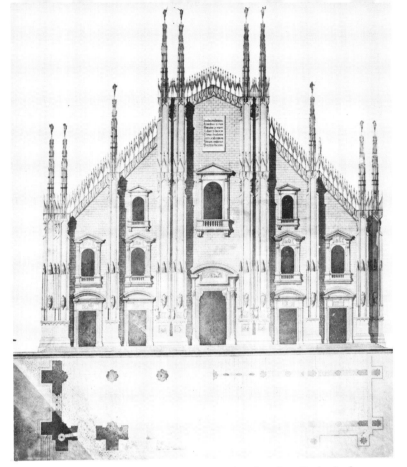

83. Luigi Cagnola. Design for the façade of Milan Cathedral. 1790.

84. Felice Soave. Design for the façade of Milan Cathedral.

85. Leopoldo Pollak. Design for the façade of Milan Cathedral.

86. Luca Beltrami. Model for the façade of Milan Cathedral. 1898.

87. Giuseppe Brentano. Project for the façade of Milan Cathedral. 1888.

IL POPOLO D'ITALIA. 20 Ottobre 1938 · Anno XVI

La decisione del Duce sul progetto Viganò

Il Campanile del Duomo
sarà pronto nel 1942

**Alto 164 metri, in marmo di Cando-
glia, occuperà migliaia di operai**

88. Vico Viganò. Project for the Campanile commissioned by Mussolini. 1938.

89. Bologna. S. Petronio.

90. Arduino Ariguzzi. Model of S. Petronio, Bologna. 1514.

91. Bologna. S. Petronio. Interior.

92. Bologna. S. Petronio. Section.

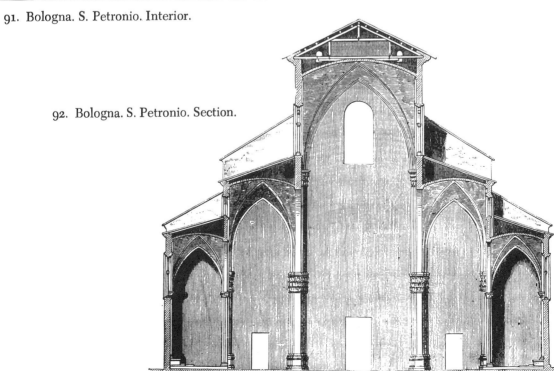

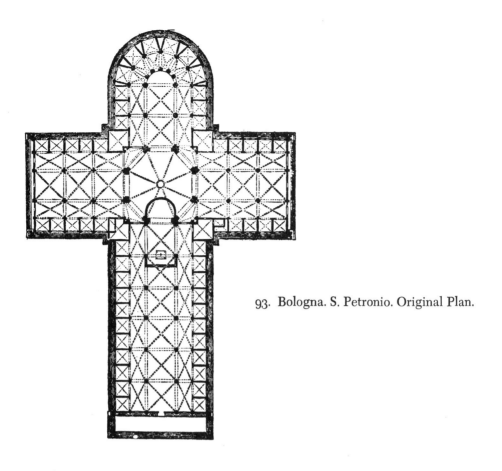

93. Bologna. S. Petronio. Original Plan.

94. Floriano Ambrosini. Model of Terribilia's solution for S. Petronio, Bologna. *Ca.* 1591.

95. Floriano Ambrosini. Model of Cremona's solution
for S. Petronio, Bologna. *Ca.* 1591.

96. Floriano Ambrosini. Section of S. Petronio, Bologna, showing the height
of Terribilia's and Cremona's vaults. 1592. Engraving.

97. Domenico da Varignano. Design for the façade of S. Petronio, Bologna. 1518.

98. Baldassare Peruzzi. Design for the façade of S.
Petronio. Bologna. 1521–22.

99. Giulio Romano and Cristoforo Lombardo. Design
for the façade of S. Petronio, Bologna. 1546.

100. Giulio Romano. Design for the façade of S. Petronio, Bologna. 1545.

101. Vignola. Design for the façade of S. Petronio, Bologna. 1544.

102. Francesco Terribilia. Design for the façade of S. Petronio, Bologna. 1580.

103. Vignola. Design for the façade of S. Petronio, Bologna.

104. Giacomo Ranuzzi. Design for the façade of S. Petronio, Bologna.

105. Domenico Tibaldi. Design for the façade of S. Petronio, Bologna.

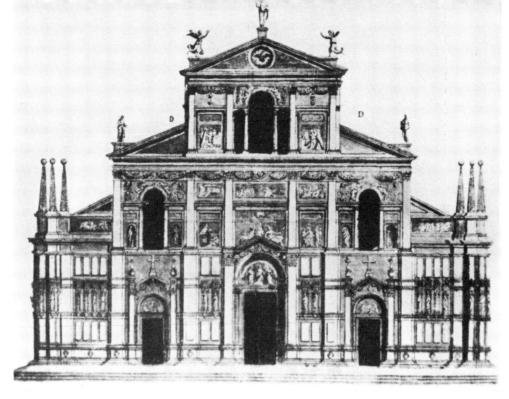

106. Palladio-Terribilia. Design for the façade of S. Petronio, Bologna. 1572.

107. Andrea Palladio. Design for the façade of S. Petronio, Bologna. 1578.

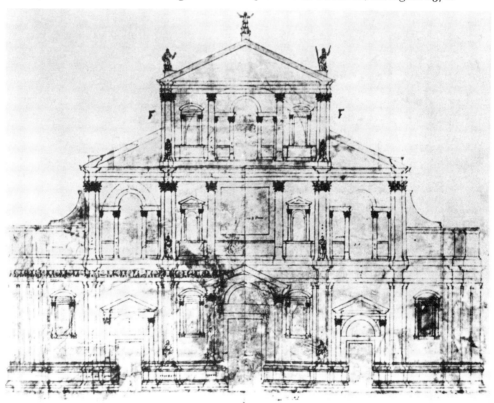

108. Andrea Palladio. Design for the façade of S. Petronio, Bologna.

109. Copy after a Palladio design for the façade of S. Petronio, Bologna. Private Collection.

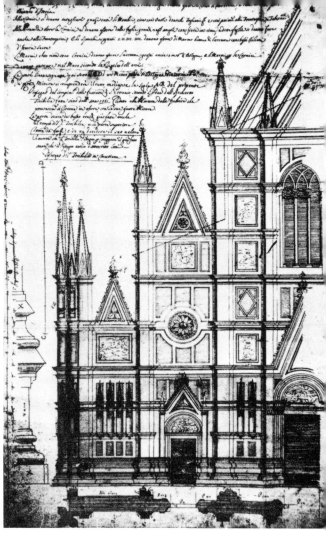

110. Carlo Francesco Dotti. Design for the façade of S. Petronio, Bologna. 1748 (?).

111. Girolamo Rainaldi. Design for the façade of S. Petronio, Bologna. 1626.

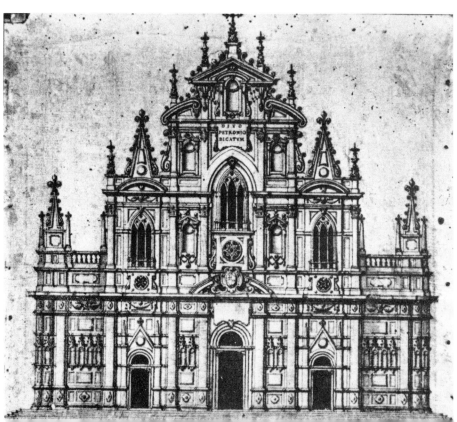

112. Carlo Francesco Dotti. Design for the façade of S. Petronio, Bologna. 1752 (?).

113. Mauro Tesi. Design for the façade of S. Petronio, Bologna. 1748.

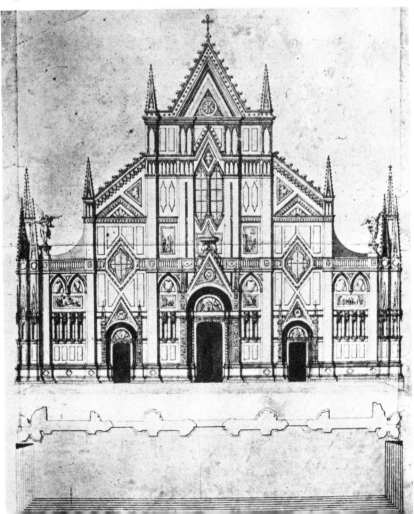

114. Florence Cathedral and Giotto's Campanile.

115. Florence Cathedral. Anonymous drawing of the old façade. 1587 (?).

116. Bernardo Buontalenti: Model for the façade of Florence Cathedral. 1589. Wood.

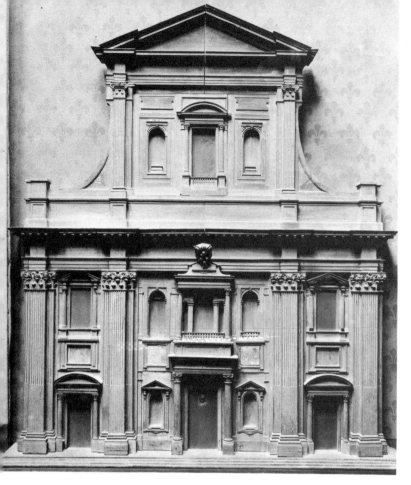

117. Giovanantonio Dosio. Model for the façade of Florence Cathedral. 1589.

118. Buontalenti or Cigoli. Model for the façade of Florence Cathedral. 1596. Wood.

119. Giovanni Bologna. Model for the façade of Florence Cathedral. *Ca.* 1600.

120. Don Giovanni de'Medici. Model for the façade of Florence Cathedral. Wood.

121. Members of the *Accademia del Disegno*. Model for the façade of Florence Cathedral. 1635. Wood.

122. Gherardo Silvani. Model for the façade of Florence Cathedral. 1635. Wood.

123. Emilio De Fabris. Florence Cathedral under construction. Before 1887.

124. Bernardo Rossellino. Pienza Cathedral. Interior.

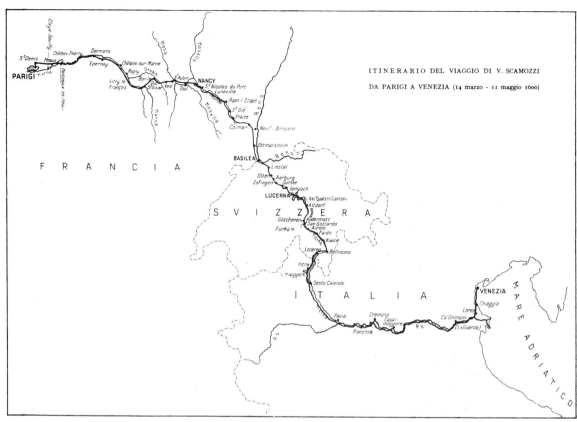

125. Route of Scamozzi's journey in 1600 from Paris to Venice.

126. Filarete. Treatise, book I, fol. V,v. Building of a primitive hut.

Sa Diomegi

Coperto d. Piombo

Gradi 127   Gradi 112   Circa P 200.

Altezza circa Piedi 130

P 32   14   18   5   24

Faccia della Chiesa

127. Scamozzi. Sketch of St. Denis, Paris.

128. Paris. Abbey Church of St. Denis before north tower removed.

129. Scamozzi. Sketch of the cathedral at Meaux.

130. Meaux Cathedral.

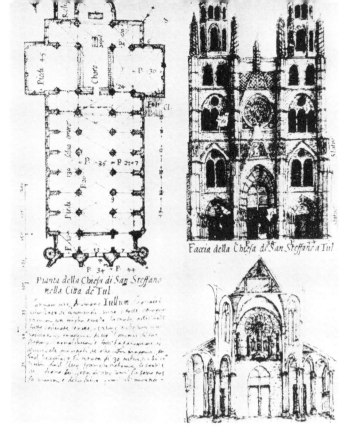

Faccia della Chiesa di San Steffano a Tul

Pianta della Chiesa di San Steffano nella Città de Tul.

131. Scamozzi. Sketches of the cathedral at Toul.

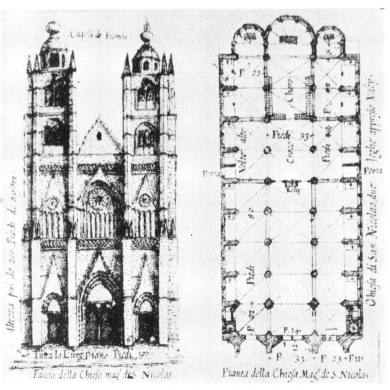

Faccia della Chiesa mag.^e de S.^e Nicolas

Pianta della Chiesa Mag.^e de S. Nicolas

132. Scamozzi. Sketches of St. Nicolas-de-Port.

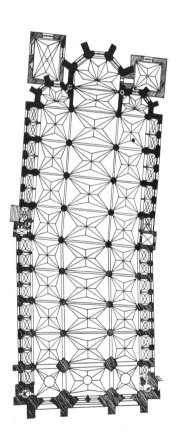

133. St. Nicolas-de-Port. Plan.

134. Francesco Borromini. Cherubims. St. Peter's, Rome.

135. Francesco Borromini. S. Carlo alle Quattro Fontane. View into the cupola.

136. Francesco Borromini. S. Ivo. Rome. View into the cupola.

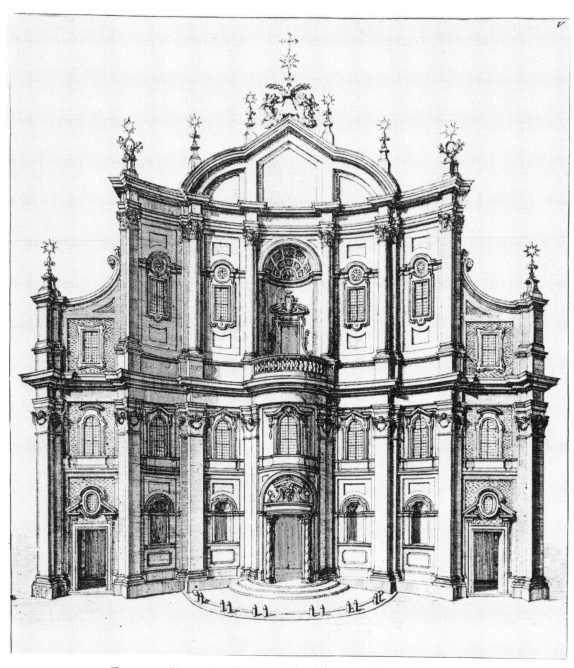

137. Francesco Borromini. Oratory of S. Philip Neri. Rome.

138. Francesco Borromini. S. Ivo. Rome. Door.

139. Francesco Borromini. Oratory of St. Philip Neri. Lavabo.

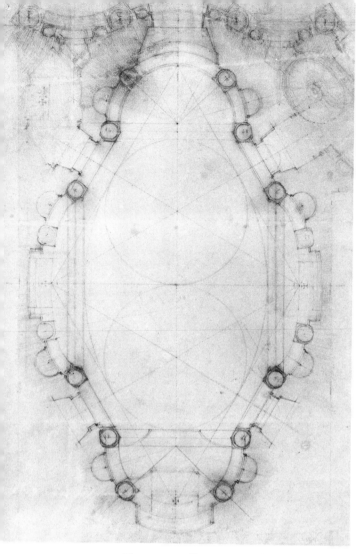

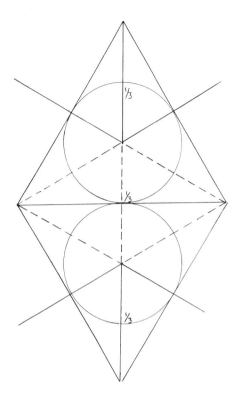

141. Geometrical Principle of fig. 140.

140. Francesco Borromini. S. Carlo alle Quattro Fontane. Rome. Plan.

142. Francesco Borromini. Sketch for ground plan of drum and lantern of S. Andrea delle Fratte, Rome.

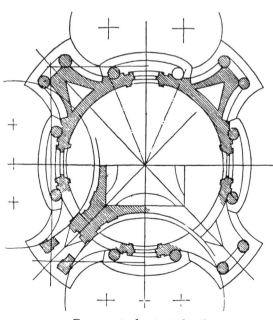

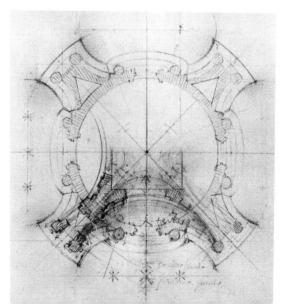

143. Geometrical principle of 142.

144. Francesco Borromini. S. Andrea delle Fratte. Rome. Drum with Campanile in foreground.

145. Francesco Borromini. Church of the Collegio di Propaganda Fide.
Ceiling.

146. Francesco Borromini. Church of the Collegio di Propaganda Fide.
Interior.

147. Guarino Guarini. S. Lorenzo. Turin. View into cupola.

148. Guarino Guarini. SS. Sindone. Turin. Section.

149. Guarino Guarini. Gothic Order.

150. Guarino Guarini. St. Anne-la-Royale. Paris. Plan.

151. Guarino Guarini. SS. Sindone. View into cupola.

152. Guarino Guarini. St. Anne-la-Royale. Paris. Section.

153. Guarino Guarini. S. Lorenzo.

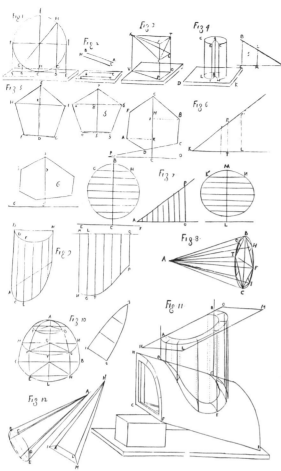

154. Guarino Guarini. Cylindrical Sections. Illustration to Trattato IV, *Architettura Civile*, 1735.

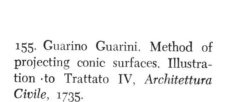

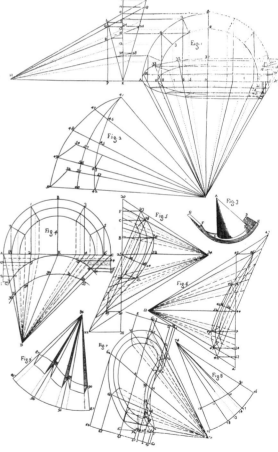

155. Guarino Guarini. Method of projecting conic surfaces. Illustration ·to Trattato IV, *Architettura Civile*, 1735.

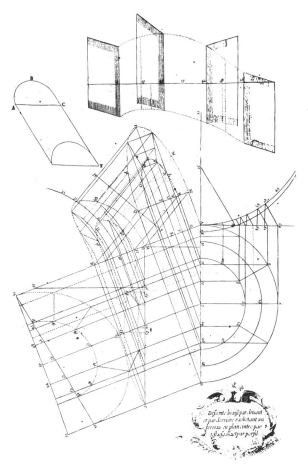

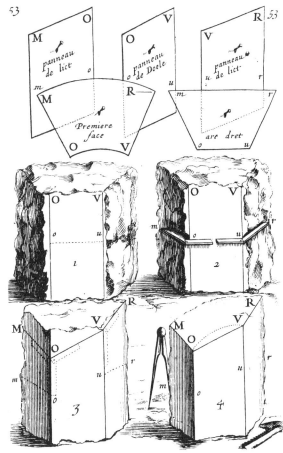

156. François Derand. Scientific Construction of Vaults. From: *L'architecture des voutes* . . . , Paris, 1643.

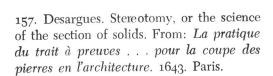

157. Desargues. Stereotomy, or the science of the section of solids. From: *La pratique du trait à preuves . . . pour la coupe des pierres en l'architecture*. 1643. Paris.

158. Nicholas Hawksmore. All Souls College, Oxford. Towers of north quadrangle. Begun 1716.

159. Westminster Abbey, London. The upper part of the towers after the design by Nicholas Hawksmore, completed after his death in 1744-45.

NOTES

The chapters of this book were read separately as lectures at the Metropolitan Museum of Art. The reader of each lecture and the date upon which it was delivered are indicated at the beginning of the notes to the different chapters.

I   THE CATHEDRAL OF MILAN: PRELUDE
Rudolf Wittkower, October 2, 1971 and Professor George R. Collins of the Department of Art History and Archaeology of Columbia University, October 21, 1972.

1. The documents are preserved in the *Archivio della Reverenda Fabbrica del Duomo,* hereafter abbreviated *Archivio.*
2. *Annali della Fabbrica del Duomo dall'origine al presente* (Milan, 1877–85), vols. 1–8 and one index vol., hereafter abbreviated *Annali.*
3. See also H. Hoffman, "Die Entwicklung der Architektur Mailands von 1550–1650," *Wiener Jahrbuch für Kunstgeschichte* IX (1934), p. 63.
4. J. S. Ackerman, "'Ars sine scientia nihil est'; Gothic Theory of Architecture at the Cathedral of Milan," *The Art Bulletin,* vol. XXXI, no. 2 (June 1949), p. 83–111.
5. See also: S. Wilinski, "Cesare Cesariano elogia la geometria architettonica della Cattedrale di Milano," *Il Duomo di Milano, Atti, Congresso Internazionale* (Milan, 1969), vol. I, pp. 132 *ff.* Hereafter abbreviated *Atti.*
6. K. Noehles, "I vari atteggiamenti nel confronto del gotico nei disegni per la facciata del Duomo di Milano," *Atti* I, p. 164, fig. 5.
7. Bramante, "Parere sull'erezione del tiburio," publ. in *Annali* III, p. 62 f. The original manuscript was lost in the fire of 1906.
8. See: L. H. Heydenreich, *Die Sakralbau-Studien Leonardo da Vincis,* Engelsdorf-Leipzig (1929), pp. 30 *ff.*
9. L. Beltrami, *Per la storia della costruzione del Duomo,* (Milan, 1887–88), p. 103; *Annali* III (6 July 1534), p. 256.
10. Ambrosiana: Miscellanea, G.D.V. no. 48. See L. Beltrami, *La porta settentrionale del Duomo di Milano* (1900), p. 22.
11. *Annali* IV, p. 67.
12. *Ibid.* pp. 67, 68.
13. *Ibid.* p. 67.

14. *Annali* V, p. 68.
15. *Ibid.* p. 73.
16. *Ibid.* p. 86.
17. *Annali* IV, pp. 88 *ff*.
18. *Ibid.* pp. 89 f.
19. *Ibid.* pp. 90, 100.
20. *Ibid.* pp. 100 f.
21. *Dispareri in materia di architettura et perspettiva con pareri di eccellenti et famosi architetti che li risolvono* (Brescia, 1572).
22. Archivio Curia Arciv. Milano, Sez. 10, Visite Pastorali Metropolitana, vol. 75, fol. 272–3; see *Atti*, III, p. 196.
23. *Annali* IV, p. 206.
24. *Ibid.* p. 220.
25. *Ibid.* p. 253.
26. *Ibid.* p. 277.
27. H. Hoffman, "Die Entwicklung der Architektur Mailands von 1550–1650," *Wiener Jahrbuch*, IX (1934).

II THE FAÇADE OF MILAN CATHEDRAL: CLASSIC SOLUTIONS AND GOTHIC VOLTE-FACE

Dr. C. Douglas Lewis, Jr., Curator of Sculpture at the National Gallery of Art, Washington, D.C., October 28, 1972.

1. *Annali* V, p. 48; N. Carboneri, *Atti* I, p. 157.
2. G. Gaye, *Carteggio inedito d'artisti dei secoli XIV, XV, XVI* (Florence, 1839–40), vol. III, p. 446; K. Noehles, *Atti* I, p. 159.
3. *Annali* IV, p. 202.
4. *Annali* V, p. 4.
5. To be found in the Registri delle Ordinazioni Capitolari, as quoted by C. Bocciarelli, *Atti* I, p. 179.
6. See, for inst., *Archivio*: A. S. Facciata e Corpo, cart. 139, 1582–1635, fasc. 36,8. On 10 July 1616 A. Bisnati and F. Mangone report to the committee on their visit to two mountains near Lago Maggiore. In one place one finds *mearolo bianco*, in the other *mearolo rosso*. The questions are: of which will one find enough for Pellegrini's projected huge columns? What will happen if the marble shows faults after it has been cut? From where does one best transport the enormously heavy load into town? The obvious waterway, the river Toce, rarely has enough water to carry such weights into the *laghetto*, the landing place near the cathedral. The expenses would be forbidding. The cutting of the marble alone, without transport, would cost around six thousand scudi.
7. *Archivio*: A. S. cart. 422, as quoted by C. Bocciarelli, *Atti* I, p. 185.
8. *Ibid.* p. 185.
9. *Archivio*: A. S. Facciata e Corpo, cart. 154, no. 6.
10. *Archivio*: A. S. Facciata e Corpo, 1518–1636, cart. 164, fasc. 2; cart. 154, no. 8.
11. See above p. 37.

12. See C. Bocciarelli, *Atti* I, pp. 175 *ff.*
13. See below p. 31.
14. *Archivio:* A.S. 139, fasc. 20, B. This is a printed pamphlet, dated Milan, 30 August 1607.
15. *Annali* V, pp. 47 f.
16. *Ibid.* p. 48; here dated 30 August 1607. The anonymous printed pamphlet in *Archivio* (A.S. 139, fasc. 20, B) has no date.
17. *Annali* V, p. 28.
18. *Ibid.* p. 164.
19. *Ibid.* p. 186.
20. *Ibid.* p. 186, 29 July 1638.
21. *Ibid.* p. 187, 26 August 1638. Buzzi received more votes than any other competitor.
22. *Ibid.* p. 212.
23. *Ibid.* p. 212.
24. *Ibid.* p. 214.
25. *Ibid.* p. 217; 13 December 1646.
26. *Archivio:* A.S. cart. 140, fasc. 22, B. 1638–86.
27. *Annali* V, pp. 218–20.
28. I.e., his "Gothic" wall strips would be infinitely less heavy and less costly than Pellegrini's giant columns (see note II–6).

III The Façade of Milan Cathedral: Gothic Designs
Professor Henry A. Millon of the Department of Architecture of the Massachusetts Institute of Technology, November 4, 1972.

1. See especially L. Marino, "Franco Castelli e il suo 'Trattato di geometria pratica'" in: *Arte Lombarda,* XV (1970), pp. 83 *ff.*
2. *Archivio:* A.S. cart. 3, fasc. 10, 1658–1812.
3. *Annali* V, p. 269.
4. See note III–1.
5. *Annali* V, p. 223.
6. Ricchino's answer was received on 6 June, Buzzi's on 12 June 1648 (*Archivio:* A.S. cart. 140, Capo XVIII, par. 2.C., no. 17 bis, 1648–51). There seems to have been a brief flurry of activity among the Deputies, caused by the foreman, who complained on 7 May 1648 that there was not enough work for the laborers unless a decision be taken quickly whether to proceed with the new or old design for the façade.
7. *Archivio:* A.S. cart. 140, Capo XVIII, par. 2.C. no. 17 bis, 1648–51.
8. See also N. Carboneri, "L'alternativa 'Romana' alla fabbrica Gotica del Duomo di Milano" in *Atti* I, pp. 149 *ff.*
9. See note III–7.
10. *Archivio, ibid.*
11. *Archivio, ibid.*
12. *Archivio, ibid.*
13. *Archivio:* A.S. cart. 140; *Annali* V, p. 236.
14. *Archivio, ibid.*

15. *Archivio:* Facciata e Corpo della Chiesa, A.S. B 1638–86, cart. 140, fasc. 27. See also *Annali* V, pp. 256–7.

16. *Annali* V, p. 285.

17. *Annali* VI, p. 119.

18. *Ibid.,* p. 121.

19. *Ibid.,* p. 124.

20. Letter by Salvi to Cardinal Albani, dated 10 October 1744. *Archivio:* A.S. cart. 167.

21. Vanvitelli was well paid for his design. On 25 June 1745 he received sixty-five hundred lire for "una sua idea nuova" (*Annali* VI, p. 144) and, according to a small account book in the *Archivio* (A.S. cart. 169, fasc. 14), another three thousand lire on 1 July. He seems to have been a good businessman who kept careful track of his expenses. He objected that the three thousand lire were paid to him in Rome by banker's order in *doppie di Spagna* [Spanish doubloons] so that he suffered a loss in the exchange, and he did not forget to claim reimbursement for such small sums as three lire for a frame for the "large design for the façade of the cathedral" and six lire for the scribe who had made fair copies of "writings in connection with the above-mentioned *veneranda Fabbrica.*"

22. *Archivio:* A.S. cart. 147, fasc. 1750.

23. *Annali* V, p. 156.

24. *Ibid.,* p. 242.

25. *Ibid.,* p. 259.

IV S. Petronio at Bologna and Florence Cathedral
Professor Craig Hugh Smyth, Director of the Institute of Fine Arts of New York University, November 11, 1972.

1. A. Springer, *Bilder aus der neuren Kunstgeschichte* (Bonn, 1886); L. Weber, *San Petronio in Bologna,* Beiträge zur Kunstgesch., N.F. XXIX, (Leipzig, 1904); E. Panofsky, "Das erste Blatt aus dem Libro Vasaris," *Staedel Jahrbuch,* VI (1930), translated as Chapter 5 in *Meaning of the Visual Arts,* Doubleday, Anchor Books, (1955); G. Zucchini, *Disegni antichi e moderni per la facciata di San Petronio in Bologna* (Bologna, 1933); G. Zucchini, "Documenti inediti per la storia di San Petronio di Bologna" in *Miscellanea di storia dell'arte in onore di I.B. Supino* (Florence 1933); R. Bernheimer, "Gothic Survival and Revival in Bologna," *The Art Bulletin,* December 1954, vol. XXXVI, no. 4, pp. 263–284.

2. Gaye, *op. cit.,* vol. III, pp. 485 *ff.* See also: Zucchini, *Miscell. dell'arte,* pp. 200 *ff.; Palladio* VI (1942), pp. 153–66.

3. Weber, *op. cit.,* p. 58.

4. Weber, *op. cit.,* p. 32; Bernheimer, *op. cit.,* p. 266.

5. Bernheimer, *op. cit.,* p. 270; Weber, *op. cit.,* p. 36.

6. Weber, *op. cit.,* p. 36.

7. Jacopo Barozzi (1507–73), called "Il Vignola" after his birthplace, was no stranger to Bologna. He had gone there, probably in 1520, as an apprentice; stayed until 1536 when he went first to Rome, then to France;

returned to Bologna in 1543 and acquired the *cittadinanza onoraria* in 1549; having been dismissed from all work at S. Petronio on 21 March the following year, he left town immediately, never to return. Although he had spent a good part of his life in Bologna, his most important works were carried out in Rome and elsewhere. Thus he can hardly be numbered among the local Bolognese artists, though he was technically correct in regarding himself as a *cittadino bolognese:* the loss of his job does not seem to have deprived him of his citizenship. (See A. Venturi, "Cittadinanza del Vignola" in *Archivio storico dell'Arte* [1889]; M. Walcher Casotti, *Il Vignola,* Università degli Studi di Trieste, 1960).

8. Fabio Pepoli's answer, dated 24 May 1579, is in Gaye III, pp. 316 *ff.*
9. Gaye, *op. cit.,* III, pp. 396 *ff.*
10. *Ibid.* p. 407.
11. *Ibid.,* pp. 446 ff.; Weber, *op. cit.,* p. 43.
12. For Dotti see A.M. Matteucci, *Carlo Francesco Dotti e l'architettura bolognese del settecento* (Bologna, 1969).
13. W. Braunfels, *Der Dom von Florenz* (Olten, 1964), p. 69.
14. L. Del Moro, *La facciata di Santa Maria del Fiore* (Florence, 1888), p. 25.
15. *Ibid.,* p. 28.
16. Indeed, here the matter rested for over two hundred years. The Florentines who had, on festive occasions, frequently adorned the unfinished medieval façade with painted canvases, felt the need of temporary decorations to be even stronger now that they were faced with a raw brick wall Thus, for the wedding celebrations of Grand Duke Cosimo III in 1661, ". . . dovendosi adornare il Duomo, si fece una facciata a prospettiva, dipinta in tela, ed applicata alla muraglia," but wind and weather soon ruined it. Another device proved more durable: "Adì 3, d'Agosto 1688 [in preparation for the wedding of Duke Ferdinand] si cominciò a fare i ponti alla facciata di Santa Maria del Fiore per unirla di mattoni, e poi dipignerla. . . ." This surface, painted with feigned architecture by Ercole Graziani, survived into the nineteenth century. (G. Richa, *Notizie istoriche delle chiese fiorentine,* [Florence, 1757], vol. VI, pp. 58 *ff.;* W. and E. Paatz, *Die Kirchen von Florenz* [Frankfurt a.M., 1952], vol. III, p. 397). The present façade (finished 1887) was built by Emilio de Fabris.

V THEORY AND PRACTICE: BORROMINI AND GUARINI; THEIR FORERUNNERS AND SUCCESSORS
Professor James S. Ackerman of the Department of Fine Arts of Harvard University, November 18, 1972.

1. Filarete's treatise is known only in copies. The original manuscript is lost. The Medici copy (Florence, Bibl. Nazionale) has been translated, annotated, and collated with other copies, by John R. Spencer, *Filarete's Treatise on Architecture* (Yale University Press, 1965).
2. Filarette, book VIII, fol. 59 r. (here condensed).
3. L.H. Heydenreich, "Pius II. als Bauherr von Pienza," *Zeitschr. f. Kunstgesch.* VI (1937), pp. 113 *ff.*

4. V. Golzio, *Raffaello nei documenti nelle testimonianze dei contemporanei e nella letteratura del suo secolo* (Città del Vaticano, 1936), p. 86.

5. G. Gaye, *op. cit.*, vol. III, p. 361.

6. V. Scamozzi, *L'idea dell'Architettura Universale, divisa in X Libri* (Venice, 1615); Reprint (Gregg Press, 1964).

7. Scamozzi I, pp. 57 *ff.*

8. In *Civiltà Veneziana*, Fonti e Testi, I (Venice-Rome, 1959).

9. Archivio di Stato di Roma, Cartari Febei; busta 72, fasc. II, insert 8; dated 16 March 1660. See: M. Del Piazzo, "Documenti Borrominiani" in *Studi sul Borromini*, vol. I (Rome, 1967); P. Portoghesi, *The Rome of Borromini* (New York, 1967), p. 433, note 26.

10. D. Frey, "Beiträge zur römischen Barockarchitektur," *Wiener Jahrb.* f. *Kunstgesch.*, III (1924), p. 87.

11. On Guarini as architect and writer see R. Wittkower, "Introduzione al Guarini" (Orazione inaugurale), *Atti del Convegno su Guarino Guarini e l'internazionalita del barocco* (Turin, 1970).

12. *Architettura Civile del Padre D. Guarino Guarini . . .* (Turin, 1737); Reprint, with introduction by N. Carboneri and notes and appendixes by B. Tavassi La Greca (Milan, 1968).

13. *Op. cit.*, Tratt. III cap. XIII, oss. prima, (Reprint, pp. 207 *ff.*).

14. *Op. cit.*, Tratt. I, cap. III, oss. nona, (Reprint, p. 19).

15. W. Müller, "Guarini e la stereotomia" in: *Atti del convegno su Guarino Guarini e l'internazionalità del barocco* (Turin, 1970), vol. I, pp. 531–574; P. Marconi, "G. Guarini ed il gotico", *ibid.*, pp. 613–635; see also W. Müller, "The Authenticity of Guarini's Stereotomy in his *Architettura Civile*," *Journ. of the Soc. of Architectural Historians* (October 1968), vol. XXVI, no. 3, pp. 202 *ff*, and W. Oechslin, "Bemerkungen zu Guarino Guarini und Juan Caramuel de Lobkowitz" in *Raggi* (Journ. of Art History and Archaeology) IX (1969), pp. 91–109.

16. Juan Caramuel de Lobkowitz, *Architectura civil Recta, y Obliqua considerada y dibuxada en el Templo di Jerusalem* (Vigevano, 1678).

ARCHITECTS OF
MILAN CATHEDRAL
SIXTEENTH-EIGHTEENTH
CENTURIES

1547 - 1567	Vincenzo Seregni 1509-94
1567 - 1585	Pellegrino Tibaldi, called P. Pellegrini 1527-96
1587 - 1591	Martino Bassi 1542-91
1591 - 1603(1598)	Lelio Buzzi 1553-1608? serves as "capomastro" and, in a provisional capacity, as Architect
1598	Aurelio Trezzi d. 1625
1604 - 1606	Aurelio Trezzi
1605	Francesco Maria Ricchino 1584-1658 "capomastro"
1606 - 1609	Antonio Maria Corbetta
1609 - 1617	Alessandro Bisnati 1582-1617
1617 - 1625	Giovan Paolo Bisnati, Alessandro's son
1617 - 1629	Fabio Mangone 1587-1629
1631 - 1638	Francesco Maria Ricchino
1638 - 1658	Carlo Buzzi d. 1658
1658 - 1679	Gerolamo Quadrio
1679 - 1686	Andrea Biffi d. 1686
1686 - 1722	Giovan Battista Quadrio 1659-1722
1723 - 1742	Antonio Quadrio
1743 - 1760	Bartolomeo Bolli or Bolla d. 1761
1760 - 1773	Francesco Croce 1696-1773: with G. A. Pessina
1760 - 1773	Giuseppe Antonio Pessina
1773 - 1795	Giulio Galliori 1715-95
1795 - 1803	Carlo Felice Soave 1740/49-1803
1801 - 1803	Giovanni Antolini 1754-1842
1803 - 1806	Leopoldo Pollak 1751-1806
1806	Giuseppe Zanoja 1752-1817: with Giuseppe Pollak, Leopoldo's son
1806 - 1813	Carlo Amati 1776 - 1852

CHRONOLOGICAL LIST OF FAÇADE DESIGNS

Names in italics indicate that designs by these architects are extant.

I

1537	*Seregni*
c. 1580	*Pellegrini*
1590	*Tolomeo Rinaldi*
1590-91	*Martino Bassi*

II

1603	*Ricchino*
1603	Pietro Antonio Barca
1606	*Ricchino* (controversy)
1607	Onorio Longhi
1607	Antonio Maria Corbetta
1608	Corbetta: wooden model
1608	*Gerolamo da Sesto De Capitaneis*
1610	*Ricchino*
1635	*Ricchino*

III

1642	*Fabio Mangone* d.1629
1645	*Buzzi*
1646	*Engravings of Pellegrini's, Ricchino's & Buzzi's projects*
1648	*Francesco Castelli* (controversy)
1652	Castelli: wooden model
1652, 1656	Bernini's intervention
1653	*Buzzi*

IV

1733	Juvarra
1733	Francesco Villa
1733	Cesare Pagani
1734	Francesco Croce
1734(1745)	*Carlo Giuseppe Merlo*
1735	*A. M. Vertemate Cotognola*
1745	*Vanvitelli* (controversy)
1746	*Gio. Battista Riccardi*
1746	*Bernardo Vittone*
1754	Paolo Gruppo

V

1787	*Giulio Galliori*
1787	*Leopoldo Pollak*
1790	*Carlo Orombelli & Luigi Cagnola*
1791	*C. Felice Soave*
1797	Wooden Facade Model
1805	Leopoldo Pollak
1807	*Carlo Amati*

INDEX *

* *Name and place index compiled by the editor.*

(188)

SOURCES OF ILLUSTRATIONS

Numbers refer to figure numbers.

Albertina, Vienna: 140, 142

Anderson: 89, 115, 144

Archivio della V. Fabbrica del Duomo, Milan: 9, 16, 19, 33, 35, 36, 47, 56, 57, 58, 60, 69, 70, 71, 72, 77, 78, 80, 81, 82, 83, 84, 85, 87

Archivio Istituto di Storia dell'Arte Lombarda: 11, 12, 14, 16, 17, 18, 28, 32, 34, 37, 38, 39, 40, 41, 45, 46, 48, 49, 50, 51, 52, 53, 54, 55, 59, 62, 63, 64, 65, 66, 67, 68, 73, 74, 75, 76, 88

Art Bulletin, 1954, vol. xxxvi, p. 280, pl. X: 90

L. Beltrami, *Per la storia della costruzione del Duomo*, 1887–88: 10, 22, 86

J. Blaeu, *Civitatum et admirandum Italiae*, Dutch ed., 1724, courtesy Avery Library: 44, 61

F. Blondel, *Cours d'Architecture*, 1698: 29

Brogi: 4, 5, 91, 114, 116, 117, 118, 119, 120, 121, 122

E. Carli, *La città di Pio II*, Editalia, Rome, 1966, pl. 29, Interior of cathedral: 124

Cesare Cesariano, *Vitruvius*, 1521: 23, 24, 25, 26, 27, 141

Codex Atlanticus, fol. 130r-B: 31

Codex Trivulzianus, M.S. 22B: 30

Columbia University, Dept. of Art History and Archaeology: 1, 2, 8, 15, 130, 133, 145, 146, 159

Columbia University, Ware Library: 6, 7, 123

F. Derand, *L'Architecture des Voutes*, 1643: 156

G. Desargues, *La Pratique du traité à preuves . . . pour la coupe des pierres . . . ,* 1643: 157

Filarete, *Treatise,* courtesy John R. Spencer: 126

Gabinetto Fotografico Nazionale: 42

Guarino Guarini, *Architettura Civile,* 1737: 148, 149, 150, 152, 153, 154, 155

A. de Laborde, *Les monumens de la France . . . 1816–36*: 128

von Matt, *Basilica di San Pietro*, 1958, fig. 16: 43

Museo di S. Petronio: 94, 95, 99, 102, 113

K. Noehles: 28

Opera del Cav. Francesco Borromini cavata da suoi originali, 1725: 137

P. Portoghesi, *The Rome of Borromini*: 134, 136, 139, 143, 147, 151

Royal Commission on Historical Monuments: 158

Villani: 13, 96, 97, 98, 100, 101, 103, 104, 105, 106, 107, 111

Vincenzo Scamozzi, Fondazione Cini, *Taccuino di viaggio . . . ,* (pl. I, IIA, V, VII, and itinerary in the book): 125, 127, 129, 131, 132

Warburg Institute: 138

R. Wittkower: 3, 20, 21, 79, 110, 112, 135, 141

G. Zorzi, *Chiese e Ponti di Andrea Palladio,* Neri Pozza, 1966: 109

DATE DUE

GAYLORD   PRINTED IN U.S.A.